THE BOOK OF RESEMBLANCES

2

Intimations

The Desert

ALSO BY EDMOND JABÈS
Translated by Rosmarie Waldrop

The Book of Questions

VOLUME I
The Book of Questions
The Book of Yukel
Return to the Book

VOLUME II
Yaël
Elya
Aely
El, or the Last Book

The Book of Dialogue

The Book of Resemblances
The Book of Resemblances (VOLUME 1)
Intimations   The Desert (VOLUME 2)

EDMOND JABÈS

The Book
of Resemblances

2

Intimations
The Desert

Translated from the French by
ROSMARIE WALDROP

WESLEYAN UNIVERSITY PRESS
Published by University Press of New England
Hanover and London

Wesleyan University Press
Published by University Press of New England, Hanover, New Hampshire 03755

Le Livre des Ressemblances II, Le Soupçon   Le Desert was originally published by Editions Gallimard.

Sections of this book have appeared in *Eolia, Epoch Hole,* and *Manhattan Review.* An earlier version of "The Book or The Four Phases of a Birth" was published in *Performance in Postmodern Culture* (ed. M. Benamou/C. Caramello), Milwaukee: Coda, 1977.

The translator would once again like to thank the author and, especially, Arlette Jabès for their invaluable help and suggestions.

CONTENTS

Intimations   5

   The Eye   9

   The Word Before the First   11

   The First Word   12

   Summits of Silence   18

   The Lie of Origins   20

   The Innocence of Creation   21

   Limits   24

   The Reception or The Impropriety
     of Place   29

   Repetition or The Future of
     the Tale   33

   The Letter   34

The Little Book of Subversion
Above Suspicion   37

   Door, I   41

   Door, II: *The Answer Averted*   43

   Roof, I   49

   Roof, II   51

   Wall, I: *The Question*   54

Wall, II: *Mouth, Voice, Power* 56

Place: *Place, Non-Place, Other Place* 58

Duration 59

The Body 61

The Book or The Four Phases of a Birth 65

On Humor 85

Whose Seal Cannot Be Broken 87

Born Viable 89

Thought, Death 91

On Blankness, I 93

On Blankness, II 96

On Blankness, III 97

The Lost Book 98

Here, the End 101

The Desert 103

Prey to the Desert Wind 105

Before the Desert 108

After the Desert 110

The Second Trial 113

We saw how words assembled, by and by, into one single manifestation of shared hope. Thus we had an *intimation* of the book.

We saw later how the book was but the letters of each word, and how this alphabet, reused thousands and thousands of times in different combinations, slipped through our fingers like grains of sand. Thus we became aware of the infinite presence of the *desert*.

*

"If it is true that within every word another word trembles to be born, look, listen how inside the word SEUIL, 'threshold,' there struggles the word SEUL, 'alone.'

"Thus you are alone at the deserted threshold of the Book," wrote Reb Assayas, who took pride in living in words.

And he added: "We can never cross the threshold of the book. It is a boundless desert."

But had Reb Zaccari not written: "Where is the threshold but in each of the six sandy letters of the word DESERT?"

And Reb Sullam: "What is a book but a bit of fine sand taken from the desert one day and returned a few steps farther on?"

1

"Who spoke before You, Lord, whose Name is innate rejection of language?" Reb Chouchan had written.

And Reb Chalem: "Before You, there could be no word. After You, what word is still possible?"

2

"My books should be read one after the other, in the order they were written, thus copying the way seconds work into minutes, and minutes into hours.

"Thus my life in the book will have asked of you only a few brief moments of reading,

"but of me, how many toilsome mornings and nights, ah, how many years of torment and doubt?" he said.

"I have placed resemblance so high that now I dream only of resembling eternity," he said. And added: "Eternity and its humble mirror, the moment."

"*I, You* are haunted by resemblance, *He* is insolent challenge, an intruder," he also said.

We were struck by how he paraded his resemblance to the man he tried to be, so much did the one we took him for resemble a man he no longer was.

Resemblance goes to the most hurried, the last.

With its fortuitous matches, it encourages the amorous foreplay of death.

O lure of nothingness.

Intimations

"Does day resemble night, and night, day, in mutual dependency, just as the word resembles silence, and the universe its absence, to the point of sameness: a day of night, a night of day?

"The instant adds its intimations to ours.

". . . intimations of voracious light at the edge of evening; dizzying chasm of dark in the purest noontime," wrote Reb Aboulbaka.

. . . this invisible crack that will one day destroy the wall.

"One bolt of lightning is enough to disfigure the sky. Then the infinite resembles a wounded man as God resembles us in the inflected emptiness of our death.

"O jeopardized circle!" Reb Hamoun had written.

Resemblance is the tragic—or comic—image of nothingness.

It is in unassignable death that we resemble one another.

"These intimations . . ."

"What do you suspect me of? I have come without ulterior motive. I wanted to see you again, chat a little . . ."

"I would like to believe you. And yet, your words . . ."

"Have I said something to offend you?"

"No, not really. But behind your words, those others, as if you were reading. Drawing them from a book, one might say."

"What words? What book?"

"We have always been frank with each other. You know all about me. Have I ever betrayed you?"

"I begin to feel . . . In fact, I suspect . . ."

"What do you suspect? Explain."

". . . precisely this book whose pages fill with words as ours vanish into the air."

"What mysterious pages are you talking about? Are we writing? There is no paper on the table to abet us, no pen between our fingers."

"We are reading; this much is undeniable. All we need do is observe each other. Just follow my eyes the way I have followed yours from the moment you came into this room. We talk with the words our reading lacks.

"What we thought we said was hiding what we perhaps tried to express, but did not reveal."

"Are you insinuating that we have not talked at all?"

"Silence is inside the word as something to be read. A book is forever to be lost."

"Your book?"

"Perhaps the book erased so many times that only a mere inkling of it is left."

"The book of our silence, the desert."

"Yes, they are like sand, those soft, crumbly bits of eraser around our deleted words and in the end, O treacherous light or, rather, wound, the stubborn, mad hope of a possible bond, this perverse worm, this maggot in the sun.

(Every word mimics its likeness within the unlikeness where it is confined.

God died of wanting to be without likeness, of pushing likeness steeped in itself to unchallengeable perfection.

The scream tears through likeness.)

THE EYE

"You should get used to regarding words as eyes that regard you," Reb Assayas had noted.

"An eye is a word that opens and closes on itself," said Reb Bahari, "that is to say, on all the words that inhabit it."

"Which words are those?" asked Reb Bittar.

"All the words that it alone feeds as well as those it secretly shares with others nearby, also with unfamiliar words that it feels coming, that it claims, and that will metamorphose it.

"Before it could dim and fade into the night, I caught the eye of the last word in my master's recent writings, and I was shaken. This word was a good-bye to all the words it had not been able to come near."

"Two survivors—the same word?—allow us to see again the buried book of days.

"Black or blue, below the forehead, they shine with what they name.

"To these words we owe our ability to read, within our books, the lost book they have read or are still reading," wrote Reb Moshem.

And Reb Alsel: "I read. My eyes plunge into the human eye of words.

"Ah, how many faces that used to people the book are now reduced to eyes?"

"Effaced, forgotten faces, but whose eyes pursue me. Words come in pairs. A solitary word is the eye of a one-eyed man," Reb Ayoum had once written.

"All these eyes within an eye . . ."
　　　　Reb Siloun

*(Innocence is the daughter of silence. It dies with
the first word.*

Innocence is never more than astonished silence.
*The eye takes one and the same look at life and
death: ours.*
*We are all born from the hollow of a word. We
shall die of a word hollowed out.*

*"I am the person I see through Him who sees me.
O transparency of God!*
*"I shall forever be that word of the book that I first
turned into a changeling," Reb Sabban had written.*

*All birth is an advent of eyes, a chance for irre-
proachable resemblance. Law of the circle.)*

THE WORD BEFORE THE FIRST

"O Law, I have given you a word as husband, knowing that this word was me," Reb Chitrit had written.

"Could it be that God is the word before the first, which can be read only after the last?

"Then there would be a language of God that man could not use before his death.

"Then death would perhaps be but a disciplined return, through the divine vocable, to a post-origin that swallows all origins. And the book, its irrefutable proof," Reb Shouker had written.

"We must not ask God: Who is God? He would not understand.

"We must not ask God: Who is not God? He would not admit it.

"We must not ask God: What is God? He would laugh," wrote Reb Somekh.

"You always speak from a silence on which you will break.

"Behind and before us, there has always been but one and the same silence: the first one," Reb Yahid had written.

THE FIRST WORD

1

If a word takes your life, it means you have a life to give.

Any word is death's challenge to itself, its only chance to die to its name,
to all the books of its name.

The word takes death at its word.

*

Man defines himself through a certain resemblance, which is his surety as well as his hope.

You comment on a book that is not the one you read, but the one you appropriate, a book that resembles the book you read.

"Does writing mean undertaking an ultimate reading, first in our mind, then through our own vocabulary, of a book whose necessity is our reason to be?

"In this case, the first vocable would be the expected, hoped-for herald of all books. It would stand out as the rallying point and one chance of countless words that, by following, would also become visible, readable.

"Because of it, the page will never have been blank.

"And therefore it immediately arouses our suspicions—suspicion that there is a book already written within the book we write, and that its sudden appearance betrays innocence where silence used to reign," he said.

> *("There is no silence," he said elsewhere, "for there is no innocence in death."*
>
> *. . . elsewhere; that is, through the detour of an unforeseen path that we would follow to the letter.)*

Something is afoot, is organizing, is preparing to function while, unawares, we stay glued to a word, a sentence, and what we try to formulate blurs and fades.

Something that is, perhaps, what we fear most.

*

This was recalled, remembered, I am thinking of it now. Where did the words lead, the silence? Perhaps right here.

Men and other voices; women and their lack of power. Streets, a desert, and memory like a slot machine that one fine day, a day of incredible luck, suddenly spits out a month's worth of coins, a year's, a century's—or several—for immediate use. Our whole past—and the past before it—in this miraculous gift of copper or silver: a fortune to be wasted as fast as possible.

I remember. Not as clearly as I would have wished nor with enough details, but as if I relived these moments in the same way, of course, and yet differently. As if they were happening right now and yet remained what happened on a certain day, a certain night. Strange! So the book with its past—or many pasts—of a book takes on body, reclaims its first body, its forgotten—or if not forgotten at least temporarily lost—voice, its bewildered, explosive voice facing a new silence more ancient than the old one, but contemporary with the mute hell of days, the faulty shell of nights.

This was recalled, recorded, I think, but where, when? A tribe, a family of words with offspring, with ancestry—so that we cannot distinguish father from son, daughter from grandma. Rejuvenated words, changing, yet loyal to their purpose, to the old ambition of letters, roughness or harmony of their rearranged and nevertheless similar sounds. Names hated, feared, loved, mourned, welcoming or distant.

And my name without other reality than the book written in its shadow waiting to be swallowed by the shadow of what is already written or still to be.

*

(To delve deep into ourselves in search of identity, what an illusion! There is no continuity in being. Everything within us is laid waste, O layers upon layers of ashes!

Only the moment can be approached in its resemblance to the moment past.

Who am I? —Perhaps the face of a moment following adventurous faces, perhaps the forgetting of all faces in favor of a single one; but which?

To resemble . . . does not mean to become the other, but to let the other be you, to some extent. It means to perish doubly with him and doubly live his death through one subjective bond.

And moreover, as if suddenly, while we labored to reduce our differences, the insidious angle of resemblance made us more keenly aware of our unbearable solitude.

"Oblivion is the end of resemblance or its beginning," he said. "Once the mask falls, the enigmatic face is reborn."

Face of life shaped by death, the artist: our face.

"Ah," he said, "if I push ever deeper this descent

into myself, it is to face, one to one, all the faces that were mine and have carved wrinkles into my forehead and cheeks.")

*

Time measures only time, but measures itself against eternity.

The eternity of time is perhaps only time's eternal return to a time that repeals it, the repeal becoming an eternity of time without common measure: frightening infinite.

All writing accepts its time, its time's rhythm, lets it permeate— as when taking a train or riding horseback—; becoming the writing of its time.

Thus there is perhaps a time of the book delivered of the time it excludes, which would be but opening wide its vocabulary.

Our glances, our least gestures create a time opposed to time, which they do not, for all that, want to reduce.

Time of creation, of submission to creation, which historical time will in the end take care of, loyal to the moment.

The time of the vocable is neither past, present, nor to come, but time *exceeded,* as one can say that a lining come undone exceeds, at a particular spot, the edge of the garment.

Time of expression. Time of extremes.

And as if we wrote only at the borders of a defective book we never open, yet fill with symbols the extravagant margins of its excessively large pages.

"O darker night within night. At this universal depth, the word blooms," he said.

. . . the greater force we feared: this promise.

*

Between book and book, in that empty interval, someone breathes, gets upset, calls, especially calls, screams, screams especially for help, as if he would be heard, as if he could be, as if his cries and screams were audible;

someone who is but a memory of someone, a wound, a love of someone now without memory, without wound, without future: a knot strangled in the too tight knot it has slung, a void scoring the void, a breath flagging in indifferent space, a wreath of smoke already hundreds of miles from the fire and still drifting until it is no more than regret of its flames, its folly and misfortune.

> ("God is the burning Book, and I am only smoke of words.
> "Divine day lies beyond all reassuring mornings," Reb Labban had written.)

2

"By a word we live. By a word we die. And we have not the least power over them," wrote Reb Saffir.

And elsewhere: "I am aware, Lord, that I am but a word You could at any time blot from the Book."

Had not Reb Achir written: "With the word CREATION, God created man. Will He with the word DESTRUCTION annihilate him?"

"We had to reinvent for ourselves the words God used to invent us. Hence our inventions have little surprise for us. Through their mediation, life and death have become natural," Reb Ayoub will write later.

The moment, like eternity, is in a word.

> ("Let me grow and die with the words of my race. I am a Jew on the strength of the first word," wrote Reb Sabban.

And Reb Eshkol: "Words, we are one and the same people."

"My people of words," said Reb Ezzin, "how sweet to our eyes, how hostile to others, so much have you suffered from their tendentious reading!

"Immense, the book of our deserts, O word exhumed from red centuries to red centuries."

And he added: "If our pages are of incomparable whiteness it is to dazzle and scare off all inexperienced readers. But it is also an eminently charitable gesture to hide from our impatient eyes, for a moment, the drop of blood we shed and whose sudden sight would frighten us."

"Our lips know Your Book, O Lord," wrote Reb Somekh, "but which brotherly hand will come and turn the pages of ours? We live in that hand's shadow."

"My life is nearing its end, my life is nearing its end," wrote Reb Choueka, "and I don't seem to have lived.

"All by myself I pull the death of my people, wagons and wagons of ashes."

And Reb Akham: "We are waiting for the Messiah. Our words hang on his unfamiliar words.")

SUMMITS OF SILENCE

She had come to me as if she suddenly felt a need to confide, but we were both without words, without gestures; dead within ourselves with a death so old it was more than just ours.

We had climbed so many steps together that now only a few were left between us and the void: sky of closed eyes, end of a life; *summit,* that is to say, the sum of all silence . . .

("The light of day needs a whole life to be extinguished. Ah, night is indeed its death," he said.

And added: "The coming day is already distinct from the preceding one by starting at its peak.")

"Ever so light, you climb
Without a word we might
recognize each other by.
It's very high, he said, the place
where we shall die."

("Going up, is that the goal?
"No danger of falling.
"We'll croak in outer space."

He also said: "A tune of silence," as he might have said: "an eternal, monotonous melody from the far end of time.")

Without proof, where words are lacking, where they are but crumbled walls, buried doors, roofs blown off.

And powerless,
because silence is the inevitable consummation of time.

. . . because the time allotted is the slow consummation of man.

("There is no time without man."
Reb Hassim

*"Drunk with eternity, disenchanted, man, whose
every bone is a prison bar, could only come up with
time, this other jail."*
Reb Tafchit)

Minutes stained with saliva and blood. At which of you has God deigned to look even once?

Whatever ends tells the unending of the end rejected.

THE LIE OF ORIGINS

Origins are perhaps only the burn of their erasure.

For centuries, I have lived in various periods of our history. I have forgotten places I lived in as well as those I only passed through.

Of my past, I have kept only a few sentences taken from unfindable books, a few rare words I perhaps said or kept secret.

As fast as memory can bring them back, my pen grabs hold of them.

"Who am I? —You might as well ask the mirror to answer for the universe it mirrors," Reb Abet had written.

We were sitting next to each other. It was already almost dark in the room. She got up, stared at me for a moment as if she did not recognize me, then left without a word.

My lips still hold the taste of her lips. I cannot help knowing that she has been, that I existed.

THE INNOCENCE OF CREATION

"Good: that we can be alive. Evil: that we are mortal," Reb Nessif had written.

There is no place to begin but the beginning of an unfixable place always to be intended, to be ended.

As a step is always but the hope—the risk, the wound—of the step to follow.

God is born of God, as light was born of light and, later, night of a night in love.

Shadow within light and light within shadow, the half-light—which gives rise to suspicion—betrays and confounds its divine duality.

God can only live in God, as death in death.

A living God—with the living flesh of a creature—is inconceivable because it would posit a beginning for God.

Beginning is a human invention, an anguished speculation about origins.

Animals—like plants—do not likely have even an inkling of it.

Living, from this point of view, would mean becoming aware that there is eternal recourse against expiring in our very ignorance of death, which God shrouds in mist to help us.

("Commencement, 'beginning': comment se ment? How does the beginning lie to itself in order to compel recognition as beginning? How does it, in lying to itself, lie to us and establish its lie so firmly it makes us believe we begin with it? This is my inquiry for today," wrote Reb Saadoun.

And Reb Assoud: *"Innocence of creation, but not of God. For He was never, at any time, created."*

And elsewhere: *"No attribute fits God.*

"If He were wise—the Wise—He would have been the advent of all Wisdom; if just—the Just—the advent of all Justice; if saintly—the Saint—the advent of all Sainthood. But God is a stranger to all birth, a stranger to the Name.

"Therefore you shall be wise with your own wisdom, just with your own justice, good with your own goodness, strong with your own strength, poor with your own misery, alone with your own solitude, by His will."

And Reb Hassoun said: *"God is Light and, like light, transparency of fire."*

And had not Reb Marsan written in the eighth century: *"God is unfathomable light, fiery beginning of all beginning of fire?"*

And, in a second treatise: *"A fire broods in every birth. You may call it SOUL, the fatal flame enclosing in order to consume them all."*)

God, like the word, is without qualities.

("A page of dark on a page of light and so on ad infinitum, this is what our books are," said Reb Assouad.

"Out of Your book, mine will be born tomorrow. Thus You shall be my reader, Lord, as I have always been yours," Reb Assam had written.

But Reb Salsel replied: "There is no Book of God outside the book of man.

"It is your own book, Reb Assam, that you read in God's.

"Did not Reb Hakim write: We try to read the book of God and, from the first word, realize that it is our own book God invites us to decipher?")

LIMITS

Facing man, there is man.
Facing God, nothing.

A dimension is needed for love and hate.
God is without dimension.

Unique, He is without desire.
He does not even know the desire of Nothing for
Nothing that torments death.

"We can only talk of dimensions because we have
an intuition of our limits."

Reb Kassim

"Do you know what they say? Ah, without rhyme
or reason: that the place where I live is no place because it does not have the same dimensions as theirs,"
reported Reb Harga.

Whereupon he was told that something outside the
human scale cannot win the approval of men.

Was this not the case here, of his place?

1

We struggle within our limits.

The unlimited undoes all limits, and hence is our undoing.

What outstrips you outstrips your reflection too. Outstripped, you are stripped of substance, as in death.

You think because you are mortal. Thinking can only be mortal thoughts on mortality.
God is without thought.

"We have loved each other, Sarah, because we are mortal and your love is a mortal love of this our mortality," Yukel had written.
And Sarah: "How great our love, Yukel, for being bound to death with every fiber!"

2

"It is always sense that is in question. It is against abuses of sense—abuse of the power its authority exercises over sense—that we work.
"Thought sustains and encourages us. We must deliver words from the sense people want to lock them into, which is always only one of the many senses a word claims in order to die.
"Thus no text is prisoner of the same reading," wrote Reb Alban.

And added: "Mine the text so as to read it beyond its death."

To open sense to sense, without respite.
To obey the word means going from murder to murder.

3

*("The infinite excludes all improvisations of the fi-
nite, just as eternity crosses out, with one unbounded
pen-stroke, the moment expressed in all that it ex-
presses and valid only at and for the moment it oc-
curs.*

*"If we speak of the infinite goodness, the infinite
justice, the infinite wisdom of God, do we not wipe
out these virtues' reason to be, their claim to serve as
example for man, who cannot grasp or practice them
except within the definite time allotted him? And who,
above all, can only with precise motives, hence only
on occasion, behave toward others as a wise, good,
or just man?*

*"We live, act, speak only in the name of a finitude
to which we are bound in all we enact or are enacted
by. For it gives meaning to our actions, our hopes,
our behavior.*

*"To act from desire for the infinite, in relation to
this very infinite, makes no sense.*

*"Eternity, like the infinite, is cut off from the sap,
is but oblivion in oblivion, sky blue in the blue sky,"
he had written.)*

4

"All you write is written in limits, within your limits. Every page allows you to measure them against those you will never know," said Reb Yachoua.

Wisdom shows us the limits where madness begins; goodness, those where evil approaches; justice, wherever injustice reigns; faith, where believing is obsolete; just as quenched thirst and hunger see their borders outlined against unquenchable thirst and hunger.

"A whiteness without a shadow of white, this is God," Reb Rafad had written to his teacher, Reb Fahim, who replied: "Does God know doubt, anxiety, despair? If I answer: No, I have grounds to conclude God did not create man. If I answer: Yes, then God is not God." And he added: "Stop wanting God to resemble what is best and worst in yourself. God is, beyond our insignificance, the non-sense implanted in any beyond."

"It is not God you exalt in His Wisdom, but your idea of Wisdom, which you would like accepted by all.

"It is not God you celebrate in His Goodness, but the idea Goodness inspires in you, and which you would like shared by all.

"It is not God you aggrandize in His Justice, but the idea you have formed of Justice, and which you attribute to Him.

"You impose resemblance on an uncomfortable relation without beginning or future with what is—for being unable to be, O night of nights—the outrage and strength of its inconceivability, the unnamable emptiness of the interstellar void," he said.

But people retorted: "What is not, is always behind: a color behind color, a sound behind sound, a glance behind glances.

"White is most likely this color; infinite silence, this previous sound; and emptiness, this open eye."

"God has no tears," he had admitted. "Man is alone to weep for man and for God."

"All my life I have coveted a place in the sun. Soon all the humid dark down in the earth will be mine," wrote Reb Zaradel.

No step escapes the preceding step.

"The road of life is straight as an 'i' topped by a point it cannot ever join, which makes it legible to us," he said.

5

("*I am inclined to think that our nothingness and God's do not at all have the same scope. One envelops the other. We must see them in this perspective,*" *wrote Reb Hamouna.*

And added, in order to illustrate his remark: "Imagine day engulfing the night, then night engulfing the day. All we shall ever be is nothing within nothing, a circle within a circle.")

And if God were the smallest circle?

Then writing would mean making God enter into the partially explored field of our limits.

THE RECEPTION
or The Impropriety of Place

"What a success!"

"Yes," I replied evasively.

The gentleman who addressed these words to me must be about my age. I do not think I have met him before.

Where were we? On whose initiative were we gathered? Neither of us seemed to know.

The liveried butler by the door, whom I could still see from my present place, seemed the only person in charge of welcoming us.

Men in white tie, women in long, low-cut dresses were crowding in, some with invitation in hand as if they suspected being the victims of an evidently fortunate misunderstanding and feared not being taken for themselves, that is, for the person invited to the reception. Some used their elbows with rare skill to clear a way to the buffet at the end of the room, drawn by the fancy dishes and drinks.

"A double-faced place," I mumbled to myself without, however, finding a good reason for my remark.

Troubled waters, rather. No. *Double* like some flowers or reversible material, with the two sides showing different patterns.

A double game is played by mutual consent. Who dupes whom? Perhaps no one.

Groups had formed according to the whims of chance. I amused myself watching them drink, eat, laugh, sing in unison. And yet . . .

"Ah, this intimation . . ."

"What intimation?"

"A silly dread, a premonition of a spectacle within the spectacle, of which we will somehow be the innocent actors. Behind these people, these voices, this setting . . ."

"Behind, there is nothing. You remember Tacitus's line: 'The secret of their sanctuary is that it is empty?'"

*

"I don't remember; have we met?"

It was the gentleman my age—or almost—of a moment ago who was again speaking to me.

"You look familiar. You look like somebody I once knew."

Why did this place fascinate me so? I might have said—but what made me suddenly think of it?—a former synagogue, profaned, the synagogue of my childhood.

In my excitement I began looking for the curtain of rare cloth embroidered with religious symbols and behind it, a few steps above the ground, the Ark of the Covenant.

I looked for the venerable scrolls in their wooden or velvet coffers inlaid with precious ornaments where the faithful placed their lips respectfully, solemnly, lovingly—for is the Torah not the bride of Israel?

I looked for the seven-branched candelabrum, the lamps with the eternal oil.

I looked for the hidden staircase to the gallery where the women retire.

I looked for the benches of waxed wood with their separate shelves for skullcaps, silk shawls and sacred books.

I looked for the lectern where the Torah was placed so that it could be seen from a distance, and be read and chanted by the congregation. Letter after letter was pointed out in its brotherly autonomy by the index finger of a tiny silver hand held by its slim stem in the translucent fingers of the celebrant.

I looked for the crystal chandelier in the center, with its thousand reflections like the broken words of an old memory. I looked for the rugs from Persia and Turkey . . .

I remember. My family used to come here to pray. Is this possible?

In front of us, a lady had apparently said something shocking to the people talking with her. She does not seem to understand why she is suddenly alone and laughs to appear at her ease, looking at me.

. . . this synagogue, desert built in the desert, full of the echoes
of centuries.

> (. . . *this desert, a synagogue built in a synagogue,*
> *full of echoes of sand.*
>
> *"A handful of sand," said Reb Acher, "is my*
> *prayer. God is closer to the hand stretching toward*
> *Him than to the mouth.")*

Let us leave. Phantoms, are you not from everywhere, whereas
we are from nowhere?

*

A place preserved in a corner of your memory and a strange party
where the guests were all anonymous, dead. With borrowed faces
and gestures they undid, knot by knot, for themselves, for all of
them, the void.

> *("In my longing for eternity I resemble death,*
> *whom I contemplate in my brothers' pale faces.*
> *"I am already older by a whole lifetime before my*
> *life," wrote Reb Siloun.)*

This place. This key, O lock of time!
We are death's guests of honor.

*

"So empty are our eyes sometimes," wrote Reb Waddish, "that
the letters of the Book can gradually invade them and, to the
rhythm of a music only they know, far from despotic words, dance
naked, dance mysterious dances in the sky."
Behind our sanctuary, there is a book and an invisible God whose

dissuasive Name is transmitted from vocable to vocable until their syllables decompose.

Thus we became the people of Nothingness, of the limpid splendor of Nothingness, through four letters that attained the silence of inaccessible crests.

. . . people of Nothingness, of the intact void on which was built the world; stone on stone, beehive on beehive, sky on sky, nothing on nothing.

("What silence everywhere," said Reb Armel. "And this crushing presence of the void. God is here. I feel it."

Nothingness is a sigh of eternity, a casual avowal of the infinite.)

The eye drowns at the first horizon.

REPETITION

or The Future of the Tale

A child, without recognizing them, says the words
of his future over and over, as if preparing to understand them someday.

Here, repetition is an apprenticeship of language.

The child talks outside time for the time when he
will finally be able to talk, that is to say, hear his
words among those of others.

A tale that goes from mouth to mouth never remains the same.
Every time, it is a new tale.

If three contradictory versions of the arrest of Sarah and Yukel
have the right to be in *The Book of Questions*, does this not force
reality to admit defeat where it anticipated triumph?

What is repeated resembles more or less—often less rather than
more—what was initially seen, heard. But how can we explain, in
this precise case, that descriptions from this same witness's pen
differ so radically?

Perhaps we are more attached to the telling than to the event it
derives from, and the telling, more than to any restrictive truth-
fulness (which is not always truth), to its own prodigious renewal,
gage of a better future.

THE LETTER

Monsieur,

I just bought your book—*The Book of Resemblances*—and it takes me back years.

First of all, I would like to confirm that Sarah's and Yukel's arrest, of which I was an anonymous witness, did happen in the way you tell it. But was it really they? This I cannot certify, the less so because it was through you I identified them. Your eyes went from one to the other, and your lips were trembling.

Before leaving France for the United States—it must have been in 1950, maybe later, or a little before; how can I know, when you neglected to mention it?—I spontaneously wrote you a letter and have been happy to read a fragment of it in your work.

How have I lived? Like a foreigner, obviously. Shall I one day learn the details of my life? I exist only through you and am thirsty for existence. Thirsty for a past and a future, which lie in your hand. You, who hate power, are here invested with a supreme power, which you are free to use at your discretion. Power to create, let live, kill, or, which at this stage is crueler yet, forget me.

Must I forever remain the person I once was, the impotent spectator of a horrible hour that still makes me want to vomit? Must I to the end of time contain this restrained revolt, this bitter disgust of heart and mind, this vomit from gut and mouth? Then have pity and tear up the page on which I belong, because I can no longer bear to take on myself alone all the shame and misery of a century in one indelible image. I was only an adolescent. Who am I today?

If I can write you it is because you have wished it, because you have a sudden need of my services. Perhaps only to let me write you this letter or—who knows?—to prepare me for a new destiny.

I must be about fifty years old. What do you expect of me? My condition, from now on, is first rights to my own life. So what have I done, said, thought since our encounter? Where have I lived, how, with whom, why? I demand to be brought up to date. But what you call the death of the book is probably our own death. So I shall not have lived, but only looked on life once, with a dead man's eyes. One moment, one everlasting moment.

Nevertheless I am not unaware that the future book, whose blank pages are concealed in the book that shelters us, is awaiting its words. May the first of them be a name, the name I implore of you, and of which I shall truly die.

The Little Book of Subversion Above Suspicion

To subvert even subversion.

. . . this sensibility of intelligence, this intelligence of sensibility, thanks to which all we understand has already been intuited, and as if shared in advance, by our senses.

There is no thought without body. Where I speak, where I am silent, my body is the body of my thought.

"Ah, the wound is deeper than we tend to believe, never completely visible," wrote Reb Souery.

To speak the language of others, but in the interrogative mode.

The door, the roof, the wall were one hole. It was all we had to wander in, to love, to die.

The relation between answer and question is essentially a power relation, hence political: relation of despotic master and slave up in arms.
Language of authority face to face with a nonauthority that only feigns to be such in order to sap authority at its base.

A marble monument might be erected for the answer; but who would think of building one for the question?
Its base is sand.

It is never the answer, but the question that sets the building on fire.

Truth always defines itself as a limit—an end in itself; the lie, as a disguise of endings—a spiriting-away of limits.

From what is to be said to what is already said, truth is the shortest way, the lie the longest.

"What characterizes truth," he said, "is shortcuts, economy of words; whereas with the lie it is detours, immoderate gab between brackets."

"Then rambling equals lying?" he was asked.

"Rambling means perhaps a truth searching for itself, hoping to amble through the book in all directions before settling at the end. The final period, point dedicated to the void on which our eyes break. Thus we understand better why, as has been said, *when God wanted to reveal Himself He appeared as a point.*"

A lie does not fall due. A lie engenders lies. Truth has truth for its opponent. It is victory or off with its head.

"What is truth," he said, "other than a dazzling lie, a diamond among pebbles?"

The roads to God are lined with diamonds.

> *(To gain on oblivion as one gains on death, unaware that any gain is a gift to the void.*
>
> *"Lord, You took all I had. But the triumph is mine. Now only my life can be taken, which belongs to You," said Reb Arias.*
>
> *And Reb Assir: "God feels affection for the man who creates. Here He recognizes Himself; for every day, this man's loss is more than a man's.")*

DOOR, I

"You come in through the door and you go out through the same door. Is this what we call life and death?" wrote Reb Aggar.

And Reb Akram: "Coming home last night I found the door locked. God keeps my key on His person. Ah, how many days and nights will He make me wait on the threshold?"

There is no door for the blind.

"Are you aware," he said, "that in going through a door you go through your soul and body? All doors are inside us.

"Life lets a little blood there, every time."

"O Sarah, we always knocked on a door locked against life," wrote Yukel.

"Inner and outer thought communicate through a bolted door. They recognize each other's voice. Death will break down this door," he said.

"Death is this door," was the reply. "For how can you explain a thought being outside or inside unless there is a border that separates life from life, that can only be drawn by death?"

When the question is without passion, the answer has no vigor.

"What is your answer?" asked Reb Areb. "I will know at which moment I was short of questions."

Yaël said: "Let this door be a flame. Then my body will learn to its cost, as my soul has, that one can only go through by displacing the fire a step."

Any question is first of all a question of fire.

Whatever is not questioned has no soul.

DOOR, II
The Answer Averted

You ask me a question. If I answer, the question will immediately be annulled by the answer it has prompted. Truly, there is no satisfactory answer to anything, even the most banal question, like: *How are you?* If I reply: *Fine,* I risk being wrong. I might die the minute after. I am forced to think of this and ask myself in turn. For answers are tied to certainty, and we can never be sure of anything. In fact, any answer engenders its own question. Example: this door. If asked: *Is this a door?* I of course reply: *Yes.* But what does this door have to do with the lonely doors of a blown-up village, with the place where they are or once were, or, again, with the portal vein?

Besides, if it no longer functions as a door, if it is definitely condemned or always open, can we still call it a door?

On the other hand, if a word insists on not-belonging by rejecting both ascending and descending lineage, if it is only, by virtue of its location on paper or in the mouth, a group of letters, a gathering of sounds that have made it a *kazak,* a stranger ousted by the tribe from which it had already split, is it not then our task to try to define its dependence on the letter, just as a soul might want to know its body? And, on this model, to define its allegiance to other groups of letters and sounds, each of which likewise forms a dissident vocable? Does anybody suspect how many words are attached to some particular word, not through sense or meta-sense, but through the five senses: their incomparably fine hearing, their sight forever tapping the invisible, their immoderate taste for ink and liquid colors, their subtle sense of smell, and above all their touch, prelude to any great adventure into the bewitching void of their truth? Body goes toward body as solitude toward solitude. And the soul is perhaps the projected desire, the invisible hyphen, the interval felt between word and word, between letter and letter, between life and death, between wound and wonder.

"Whoever is alone embraces the universe," wrote an anonymous rabbi whose old notebook I found.

The book of exile is but a book of exiled words. Exile is staked out by violence.

"Only a creature without any ties can know divine exile, because he is a stranger even to his exile," the same rabbi had noted.

True, a clear question calls for a precise answer. However, to specify precisely means most often to reduce, and you cannot reduce a word to a word.

The history of not-belonging flaunted by rebellious vocables is the history of world excluded from world and, at the same time, integrated in a universe turned aside, distracted from its future.

> *("One day I shall have to explain how this belonging of the word became not-belonging to the word or, rather, how this not-belonging came to belong: my itinerary as a Jew."*
> *"Are you Jewish?"*
> *"Will I have been? Only as the void torments the void?")*

Say more through silence? Introduce the upheaval of being silent, which we had carefully silenced at the heart of saying? Let the word bury the mirror of its likenesses or, on the contrary, brandish it till it explodes with excess of image, with diversity of significance, with the play of reflections of shattered and reshaped forms? Accept losing yourself in the work or try to save yourself? Make yours the insistence of vocabulary and face the book or trample on the book by harrying its words? This is how writing differs. And this difference is the law of distance.

[*The eye bears witness to what it sees.*
Evidence *conceals* avoidance *with* void *at the core.*
(God is) A VOID (in this word).
(I am) A VOID (in this word).
Evidence is avoidance of certainty.]

I am a man of writing. The text is my silence and my scream.
My thinking advances with the help of words, moved by a rhythm
which is that of the written. Where it runs out of breath I crumble.

(I am not losing track of your question; I am leaving it suspended.
Around it, other questions, always more, gather and regroup. It is
by gliding from one to the other that I have composed my books.
They are the sum of these questions, questioning a questioning
uninterrupted by any reply until death, which remains the ever
questioning question of death.)

The experience of the desert has been crucial for me. Between
sky and sand, between All and Nothing, burns the question. It
burns without being consumed. It burns for itself, in a void. The
experience of the desert is also one of listening, extreme listening.
Not only do you hear what you could not hear elsewhere, true
silence, cruel and painful because it seems to reproach your very
heart for beating. But also, as you lie in the sand, for example, a
strange noise may suddenly intrigue you, a noise as of a man or
animal walking, coming closer every minute or moving away, or
seeming to move away while following his path. A long while after,
if you are in the right direction, the man or beast announced by
your ears appears on the horizon. A nomad could have identified
this "living thing" immediately, before seeing it, just by ear. Of
course, the desert is his natural habitat.
    As a nomad his desert, I have tried to circumscribe the blank
territory of the page. I have tried to make it my true place, as the
Jew has for centuries tried to make his the desert of his book, desert
where the voice, profane or sacred, human or divine, encounters
silence in order to become word, that is, silent utterance of God
and final utterance of man.

The desert is much more than the practice of silence and listening. It is eternal openness. The openness of writing, which it is the writer's job to preserve.

Openness of all openness.

(I am not avoiding your question. I am going deeper into it. In doing so I see no clever dodge, but the outline of an answer dimly taking shape.)

As far back as I can remember and as much as I can be sure, I believe the spelling errors I made as a child and adolescent were the origin from which my questioning grew. I had trouble understanding that a word copied a little differently, with a letter too many or too few, suddenly did not represent anything, that my teacher could angrily cross it out with red ink and claim the arbitrary right to punish me for inventing it, as it were.

So a word did not exist unless spelled correctly, as someone—but who? God, perhaps?—had chosen, had decreed it should be spelled. Unless this so-called usage was simply a plot of the letters? And how had the letters come to have such power over man that they could lay down the law? What mystery dwelled in them? Sometimes I also thought if I spelled a word my way I could be the only one to live with it, to love it—we can only invent words of love. In a burst of fraternal feeling I dreamed of a new language for a secret society. Among my challenged vocables, I felt both free and a slave to their freedom.

("*It is in the word* JEW *that we are persecuted.*

"*If* JEW *could suddenly be spelled* JEWE *or* JOU, *perhaps the persecution would stop,*" *said an unhappy scholar to a rabbi.*

"*We would be doubly persecuted,*" *replied the latter:* "*in our alliance with the word and in its madness. God expunged the Name so it should never expunge us.*" *And he added:* "*In the permanence of this word lies our permanence, guarded by its letters graven into the infinite absence of the four divine letters.*")

I do not know if the idea of the Messiah who will come to transform the world—or to annihilate, at any rate to change it—is a
source of hope or fear for the believer. For me it represents the
idea of a great writer, because, as we face a text, what are we keyed
to if not change? And what are we exposed to but the unforeseeable
change we owe to its brutality? Messiah is also a vocable.

In our task, we are like believers buoyed up by immense hope
and at the same time shaken by unutterable fear. It happens that
a writer commits suicide at the threshold of a book. But never will
a nonwriter die *for* a word. This also, I think, is worth meditating
on.

The book remains a mystery and indefatigable deciphering of the
mystery. Life and death are faced with their own image, and this
image is a letter; so that in tracing a word we die and are reborn
in the question of its daring. Writing rejects all answers by its very
nature, which is a question asked of the question.

It is in daily attention to this question, in the notch it has cut
into them, that my books continue to be written.

What is my role in their production? They have so often rejected
me that I could not claim to have composed them. But I have at
least borne them. The crowd of characters consumed with demands
that has invaded these works has, by enlarging the field, allowed
reflection to unfold freely, allowed the question to fill the space
opened by the preceding question. A book of contradictions as
much as of affirmations torn by contradictions. But then, is thought
anything different? What is a thought but the expression of its mas-
tered contradictions in a few sentences menaced by death, or even
death itself exposed in its encrusted phrases? In thinking we follow
death on its dark road, shed light where we can, only to discover,
at the moment we manage to approach, its mysterious face of absence.

Everything dies of being thought. All thinking questions death
and is death questioned. Then conceiving of God's death would
mean attacking the Thought of thoughts which, for not dying to
itself, perpetuates its death in the *thought* of death it assumes. *God
is dead* could only mean: *God is death,* conceived in His death. He
is all the thinking engulfed in the ineluctable question of His death
which He survives without Himself.

(I am not giving up on your question. I breathe strength into it. I deprive it only of its end. But it will perish or, at best, remain nailed to nothingness for having inspired only detours.)

I have never known what people mean by a work of the imagination. Writing, as I already noted, is the opposite of imagining. Where words wield their power, writing could mean putting this power on a tried and tested base, not by sharing in the power—or palliating the lack of it—but by making sure of its organization. Afterward, everything is in the open. Everything is in process of becoming, summoned to bloom. This is why there are no codes or bars to imprison the book. There are only vast conquered surfaces as far as the written eye can reach.

The characters in my work, presented as interpreters of the book, come from all centuries. Thus my books develop outside their time as well as inside time. Above the frontiers crossed—at the end of all frontiers—there shines a sun, a question mark whose formerly most noticeable part has disappeared: the mark is now a point only, with the sense of a point of vertigo, a period whose finality goes beyond the book.

Nomadic writing. Book of the nomad.

Do I know today what it means to make a book? It seems I plunge in as I used to plunge into the desert. Back in the city I had a clear impression of coming back from oblivion.

Making a book is perhaps this: to earn oblivion.

> *("Poor us," wrote Reb Messikh to his favorite student. "We have inherited the madness of the book and there is no hope of a cure.")*

ROOF, I

"It was at the high point of our lives," Yukel had written to Sarah, "that misfortune struck us. Think of a mountaintop taking revenge on a climber's daring.

"And yet our love was simple—like a simple note, a simple flower, the simple tenses of a verb, simple like mother's milk in the infant's mouth. Simple also, alas, like the words that condemned us, like the indifference of people who looked the other way. And like truth, often incomprehensible.

"Our truth stifles us. For us, Sarah, it has been nothing but this heavy suffocation to which we succumbed.

"Do you remember how the two of us once climbed to the roof of a half-ruined house? It was in a little village in the Cévennes, shortly before the war. We had a view of the whole countryside. Up there you squeezed my hand hard and said: We are alive at the heart of our love."

"Our truth has only tried to shed the useless truth that is on our own scale, as one takes off one's clothes to plunge into the sea.

"You and I are naked, as on the first day of Creation," Reb Arias wrote to one of his disciples.

And he added: "The truth that comes from God is sovereign; but how can we know to what point it was already ours? Did not Reb Liod write: Is our relation to God perhaps only a relation to ourselves, soul to older soul?"

You said: "In our deepest memory, truth is the stubborn echo of a truth so often wounded that it is now nothing but our wound."

"Truth," you also said, "does not exist. It is like us, who, even with the light of love on us, are sheer ignorance, on which we presume as if it were warm knowledge."

"Our pain was only pain of being, anticipated happiness of a lasting bond with what cannot be bound and whose abyss we have skirted. Our union has known this vertigo," you also said.

"O Sarah, to what point were we the void of an impossible truth, to which our own truth tried to measure up by negating it?

"Every moment is a fierce battle over a page blackened with life."

ROOF, II

(We are born and die of truth as we are born and die, not for nothing, but for a sublimated idea of All and Nothing.

Some people claim to know they are lying when they tell the truth; others—most—claim not to. They are not, in any case, what is at stake, but truth as such.

Clear or obscure, our writing, brilliant or dull. Day and night share the same portion of world, the same ink.

Not telling the truth is not necessarily lying. We often lie in good faith because we cannot distinguish between true and false, because we lack the references, or even in a spirit of respectful tolerance. Truth accommodates this kind of ingenuity.

Truth has no face. Any one would fit, but truth rejects them all. Yet it always accosts us with familiar features: the features of evidence.

Truth is in essence an impossible undertaking.

Evidence, enemy of appearances, has the void for its ally.

As for truth, is the abyss all we shall ever have
glimpsed of it?)

Once truth is put down on paper it is nothing but a word wrestling with proof and counterproof, torn between them. I have long, at any rate since my first texts, watched over its weaknesses as you tremble for a beloved who has undertaken a dangerous feat. For nothing is more vulnerable than the illusory and contingent sovereignty of the truth that presides over the fate of the book.

"Caught at the game it must play to its own harm, the truth that makes us bleed is itself bleeding. It is because of its own torment that all truth torments. Hurt by it, man and world show the same wounds," wrote Reb Soued.

Truth is not transmitted, it is snatched. It is the object of all questions, their leaven and stake.

"Let your question be your truth," wrote Reb Zayad, "for without it there would be no questions, and without questions, what truth could ever convince us?"

*

All truth is hurt by the truth it carries, as a tree by its fruit and a mother by her newborn child.

The fruit also bleeds, like the newborn, from the same induced severance.

"We approach truth with scissors," wrote Reb Sakkal. And Reb Antob: "My truth, today, is my bleeding bladder."

("Truth," a rabbi admitted to his disciple, "has
been the source of my ruin, the inevitable caving in
of my roof;
"but my passion for it remains intact."

There is no question to ask of death but would be
death for the question.

No word will spread the truth. It will die of it.

With every sentence, truth erases the book within the book; for there is no truth outside it resembling this stage of intolerance, this degree of pride.)

WALL, I

The Question

A question is more stubborn than a wall.

"At the foot of which wall have I lost my senses?
At the foot of which wall have I recovered my senses?
It seems, all I've ever had as horizon was a wall," Reb
Zayad had written.

*

"The question," he said, "is like a block of cut crystal whose thousand facets, at daybreak, strike us all
at once. We must face every single one of them."

For the stranger, questions. For the native, answers.

"To question means not to belong, means, for the
time of the question, to be outside, on the wrong side
of the line," Reb Koyré had noted.
Reb Haïm wrote to him: "I have made the question
my life. Have I not then been Jewish?"
"I was referring to the median line," replied Reb
Koyré, "the one outside the bond that cuts it in two."

*

"I write *God*, and I am the word *God*. I write: *Who
God?* and am the word: *Who*," noted a rabbi with
whose thinking I used to be familiar.

"Do not listen to the man who has an answer for everything," he said. "He is in error. Investigate, there is your truth, which you don't want to accept."

There is a challenging power so absorbed in its challenges that it becomes their pathetic victim.

It never presents itself as a power, but as the sworn enemy of all such, whose power it then quickly usurps, drawing from its questioning the strength to destroy itself.

"The man who has the answer has, undoubtedly, power. Does this make the question a non-power, a negation of power? But a virile non-power whose blows would be feared?

"The question undermines the answer at its base," he said.

Could it be that the question's impotence is only its stubborn will to survive itself, its failure caused by our impotence and as if this impotence were definitely its salvation?

The salvation of the question is also that of man.

The question's impotence defies all power, which it knows to be only the feigned authority of dumb impotence.

God died of our impotence, of our interrogations which are but implacable questioning of our powerless power.

Death has rendered God unto God, and man to his tragic freedom to live unto death.

Questioning means giving ears, eyes, brain, hand, heart, and voice to the object of the question. In a word, granting it a life of dignity, happy or painful, but rich.

. . . with such riches, the universe runneth over.

WALL, II
Mouth, Voice, Power

Power, here, would only be the acquired means to provide ourselves with a bold and contagious non-power.

In this case, the voice is a passage from daring speech to silent utterance, which secretly predominates. It is the latter the book has in its keeping, and of which we do not know how much it changes us; voice that carries the brutal or barely perceptible change the writer is working, pressed by time, haunted by the absolute, another—haughty—form of power.

So the act of writing would appear to be the consecrated gesture of handing man's power over to the utterance of the book, equivalent to sacrificing the word to its power of absence, allowing it only its immediate, ill-timed manifestation.

We are born and die of this perpetuated, never deferred power. To attain it we resort to our creative force—whether friend or enemy—whose word remains center and bond. But we continue to answer only for ourselves, even where nothing remains of us, marking our power to disappear, with its intoxication as well as its despair.

No mouth but for affirming death, and no hands but ours to bury the mouth.

> (*In writing we wrestle with a part of death just as we wrestle with only part of the dark.*
> *So writing means to confront death in its fleeting*

totality, but to measure ourselves, each time, against
only one of its instants.

A trial beyond our strength, which leads us to write
against the writing of death and to be ourselves written by it.)

PLACE

Place, Non-Place, Other Place

There is no place not the reflection of another. It is the reflected place we must discover. The place within the place.

I write at the mercy of this place.

If I write: "This is the sky" on a factory or subway wall, what sense does the phrase take on?

Does every sentence have its place? And could the book be the sum of those places?

And what is a place that is itself a multitude of places?

A book is perhaps the loss of all place, the non-place of the place lost.

A non-place like a non-beginning, non-present, non-knowing, an emptiness, a blank.

. . . but what about the constellations, the moon, the sun? But what about words?

Nothing holds them back. *They are held back by themselves.*

What holds us back is writing of place.

DURATION

"Did I die before my life, or was I born after my death? I have lost all memory of the past and no longer know if it was the time of my death or my moment of life swallowed by time, the endless time of a mortal wound.

"Life knows no duration. Nothing endures but in death," Sarah had written to Yukel.

". . . it is this death, Sarah, that will have been our life, this death that one day overtook it, that we go on questioning, just as you bend over your future in order to know, not what will become of you, but what will be left of a word, an embrace, a separation that overwhelmed or frustrated us."

(Yukel's Notebook)

*

"Is it day," asked Reb Talma, "is it night? How am I to know?

"My thinking is so confused I cannot distinguish a minute from eternity, or eternity from a minute."

And he added: "Bottomless inkwell knocked over at the first gesture of divine despair. Our universe is black with ink, our stars are drowned.

"God has given up writing."

"Eternity is neither one eternal moment nor the sum total of centuries. It is the negation of time, hence its death," he said.

"God, through man, contemplates God. Eternity could be this absent glance.

"Eyes plunged into the void, I stare through God's eyes at nothingness," wrote Reb Ayoub.

THE BODY

1

And the stone said: "Is it thanks to my body, my wounds, the inescapable violence whose victim I am, that I can roll?"

And the Jew said: "Kicked like a stone, body bruised by blows, is it the boundless, gratuitous violence against me that is accountable for my wanderings?"

Heavier than misfortune are our steps.

"What are these mountains that move?" asked Reb Cherki. "You might say a world passing away in the fullness of time.

"Broken at the center, lighter than our feet, the stones of cataclysms."

And Reb Fina: "They sewed stars on our heart to appropriate our clear nights; for though we were prey to their abuse of power, deep down they knew that, transparent and vast like the sky, we could never be seized."

"You leave us, with the land of your joys and tears in back of your eyes.

"Thus, thanks to you, the earth trains for exodus.

"It was perhaps necessary that the world should one day succeed in hoisting itself to the height of despair."

2

To make the body speak. Make the guts speak. Make marrow and bones speak to exhaustion, to abandon.

To destroy thinking and vocabulary by excess of thought and words.

To founder where there is neither life nor death, but the void, the infinite void that neither life nor death can bear.

3

"Never say you have arrived because, everywhere, you are a traveler in transit."

Reb Lami

4

What world can be ours after all those we were refused? Our body is unwanted.

5

O Sarah, we had a body for each other before it became an open wound, a body for caresses and love—twofold body for ecstasy and unease.

We have—with how many of our brothers?—covered the bare

breast of the earth with festering wounds, with ashes still smoking and wounds. But no blade of grass, no tree, no road bears witness.

"Day bears witness, perhaps. Day, which blushes and veils its face at hearing our darkening names."

6

What is a young and handsome body in death? What is an old, withered body in life?
There is no body but for remorse.

7

What kills or is killed except the body?
Death knows nothing but body.

8

All roads start from the body and lead back to it.
The body is the road.

9

Death is the enemy of the road.

10

Having exhausted all roads, God is without body.

The sun drowns the universe in light. Nowhere will you find a trace of circle. Even a point here would be pointless.

Blankness of text.

THE BOOK

or The Four Phases of a Birth

1

He made this absurd statement that each letter of our name was a phase of our life, and if death haunted us day and night it was because the last letter, drawn like the others by our own hand, fascinates us with its singular visibility.

He also said, the fact that the last letter of his first name was unpronounced rather confirmed that this letter was, not dead, but a letter of death.

And added: Sometimes the letter of death separates the flourishing letters of a name.

Against the time of life granted, it silently opposes the eternity of time that is its own.)

2

If life is a tale, so must death be.

But death comes before life.

So there must be a tale before the tale, a tale underneath the tale being written—which perhaps rewrites it in the process.

Unless we live the two tales simultaneously, as one: the tale of the life of our death, the tale of the death of our life.

"On the left page of my book, you read the story of my life, on the right, that of my death," a sage, whose words I alone report, had one day said to his young disciple. "O that the story of my death could become the story of your life. Then you would reopen the book!"

3

("*Even the smallest little flame has ulterior motives of fire*," *said Reb Khayat.*

"*I have sometimes believed I was never born, so much are my past and future one with death*," *wrote Reb Bouteri.*

"*Take this blindfold off my eyes. Then I shall finally know the difference between life and death*," *cried Reb Dabbous.*

"*Like a bird in its nest, all of life takes refuge in the eye*," *said Reb Safra.*

"*O Sarah, your name on my lips is the sweetest birth*," *Yukel had written.*

"*He walks along walls at dusk.*
"*He is but the shadow he has lost.*"
                                        Reb Zacchari.)

4

"You are as old as your most remote memory."

Reb Sabban

"In sleep you have no age."

Reb Messikh

If affirmation is only the negation of a negation, if it must earn the right to be positive by forever negating what negates it, then all questioning must pass through systematic rejection of the answers it has called forth. They will serve as springboards for new interrogations. So that the question of the book, which interests us here, today, can only be a permanent challenge of the book, that is, of writing, of birth and death, truth and lie, presence and absence, reality and fiction, of what is written in it and read, of what is born with the birth of each page and dies of its death, of its truth or lie, its undefinable presence and infinite absence.

Could it be that man is a book that he can read only in the book he will write? As if the very act of writing made it possible?

My life is in the book, and the book is my life. Life that I learn to read with every moment lived beside the word that fights me for it, for the most extraordinary shared adventure.

*

Does the adventure come before the text or the text before the adventure? And what adventure is this that the text holds and forces on us until we live only its adventure, now more than any other our own?

Writing means an opening in our life, through which life is made text. Words are the stage on the road toward the unknown where the mind pays for its daring—that unknown without which our thinking would be dead rather than meant to die in the very quick, the very torture of its death.

I

I was born on April 16 of a year I do not remember. Can recalling this date serve as starting point for a long and slow digression around the book? You know that digression is my method. As if all we are ever led to express, whether with difficulty or with the greatest ease in the world, were from the start doomed to wandering, ideal prey to commentary whose tyrannical grasp we do not suspect, for it insinuates itself gradually, approaching through customary approaches. A parenthesis the word opens, in some independent way, impatient to take the gag from its integrity—once at its mercy, we do not know where it will sweep us in its wake.

In the book, nothing is said that is not, often without our knowledge, revised in the margin, questioned, cut. Nothing is said that is not a pretext for new expressions, other paths, tender or deep ties. So that trying to write anything in all honesty and loyalty would mean trying to be said by what is said, and what this *said* suppresses, cleverly rearranges, and transforms; this *said* that is itself said, hence manipulated, exploited, liberated in its turn. As if being free meant, precisely, being exploited by this freedom we claim, in whose name we declare ourselves free.

*

Going back, for example, to my sentence: "I was born on April 16," I realize, as phase one, that it was originally forced on me by its disclaimer. In *Elya*, the book we can now consider the fifth in the cycle of *The Book of Questions*, you can find the following disclosure:

> "Although I was born on April 16 in Cairo, my father inadvertently declared at the consul's office issuing my birth certificate that I was born on the 14th of that month.
>
> "Is it to this error in calculation I owe my unconscious feeling that I have always been separated from my life by forty-eight hours? The two days added to mine could only be lived in death.

"As with the book, as with God in the world, the first manifestation of my existence was an absence which bore my name."

I won't dwell on the indirect repercussions this confusion may have had on my life and certainly has had on my books—on my relating to everyday occurrences through my books, as if the daily events could find authority only in the portion of eternity they assume and are consumed by. I won't dwell on the repercussions of this confusion of my father's when about to declare day and hour of my birth, confusion all the more astonishing because he was not given to this sort of thing.

I must admit, moreover, that nobody is beyond such errors. At the time, in the Near Eastern country where my family had lived for generations, notices of birth or death could be sent in writing to the local authority, which immediately issued a certificate that alien residents handed to their respective Consuls. Did my father think he was writing April 16 while his pen shaped the figure 14? Still, he always claimed he had made the declaration in person, but since, according to custom, he had several days, even several weeks, to discharge his obligation, it is easy to see how he could make the error. Unless it was the fault of the clerk who wrote it down and was perhaps more than usually hurried or distracted that day. Which is not out of the question.

In any case, this error in calculation, which I would never consider as such, but, rather, as a chance warning, distressed me so much that I made up my own explanation. I saw it as concrete proof furnished by the unconscious *that we are older than our life.* Out of this guaranteed void, this countersigned outside-of-time, *The Book of Questions* has drawn its voice and place: universe of silence and night, burning with the pregnant forgetting of a day unassigned, unclaimed by any human being. A day that escaped the lie of light and revived in the distress death can plunge us into with its loathing to die of a truth that is only a trap set by the lie, subtle or gross. For all truth passes through the lie, which is its foundation. So we might well deduce that truth speaks through the lie it denounces, while really denouncing only itself as an apotheosis of a lie carried to the height of perfection.

Truth, which is birth, has as its opposite the death of a truth.

Both are figures of fiction, story within the story, life within the life that voids it. We are forever the tale that tells us and the daring of this tale. Told without respite, will we ever know who we are? Will we ever know which of all the stories our vocabulary regales us with was ours?

Innumerable questions agitate every question. Will we always give in to their demand?

Will we die of a question that is the unquenchable question the wave asks of the sea, and death asks of death?

Do we probe only in hope of an answer that would set off more questions? The Jews bear witness: for centuries, they have not stopped harrowing their truth, which has become the truth of the questioning that glorifies it.

God speaks behind death, at the borders of thought.

II

In its second phase, this harmless beginning: "I was born on April 16" raises the question of birth and thereby leads to the idea of biography. I shall come back to this. For the moment, however, I must stress that for nearly twenty years I have not put myself on stage, have not used the pronoun "I" in my books. Other "I"s, with whom I obviously identify, have exploded the "I," "Me," "for My part," as they have exploded the place where I am, the place I come from, and the place I am going. Is it surprising then that my works (where so many stories crowd and call to one another) are but the heeded traces of fatal encounters, traces of charred traces, scars of words discovered on closer acquaintance? Because every word has its history, which is fed by our own. Who could deny that certain obsessive words—in *The Book of Questions*, the words "God," "Jew," "Law," "Eye," "Name," "Book": God as extreme name of the abyss; Jew as figure of exile, wandering, strangeness and separation, which is also the writer's condition; Book as impossibility of the book or, rather, as the place and non-place of all possible construction of a book; Eye which means law ("Within the word *oeil*, 'eye,' there is the word *loi*, 'law.' Every look contains the law" [*Aely*]); Name as the unutterable Name, repeal of all names, the silent Name of God, of the invisible—who could deny that certain words of our intimate vocabulary are as if transparent for a story that by and by writes itself, a story most likely truer than the one we take pride living.

Why be stubborn, I once asked a novelist, why try to invent a story and make it plausible like a true story when it is enough to examine a word charged with the weight of our anxieties, our holidays, our lonely days after, one of those headstrong key words for which we are veil and face, sand and horizon, to make stories surface from the depth of memory, stories heard, found, lived? But I was probably wrong. Does writing not always mean obeying a word that haunts us?

How many dead whom we knew, cherished, or perhaps detested or despised are buried in the word DEATH. How many loves that marked our lives go on flowering in the word LOVE. Do we not already speak of ourselves when we use these words?

Then every book would be autobiographical, since the book of my name is but the history of an absent book become the book of my history.

The book would be the biographer of the book whose place it has usurped. Its own biographer.

From the mouth of an anonymous woman, probably Sarah, beloved of Yukel, who, as hero and narrator of the book, is himself both word of flesh and word of ink, each receiving life from, and losing it with, the other—from a woman's mouth we hear and read these sentences in *El, or the Last Book* which closes, without closing anything, the series of *The Book of Questions*:

". . . *écrit*, *récit*, 'written,' 'story': the same word in a natural inversion of its letters.

"'Any writing suggests its portion of a story,' she said."

Thus, in coming to light, a word issuing from the rearranged letters of a word under which it lay dormant gives us access to a forbidden reading of the former. I can perhaps make this clearer farther on, there where I am lodged, where I have always held on, and as if this "always" were only the sum of all the instants of a day forever rebegun. But this might suggest a unique day formed by all days past or future, which is not at all the case—although I am not convinced that this perpetual day might not be exactly the day of writing, day within the day or, rather, within the days. A day of such intense, such dazzling light that the rows of words can see nothing but themselves. Farther on then. But what is far where there is neither root nor end? Where farther could be behind or before me, above or beneath? It could—and why not?— be the place fixed for our facing each other in a final confrontation. Then everything would be at stake in this separation that paradoxically brings us together. How? Before answering this we must first, I think, ask: What is separation, what does it mean to be separate?

One eye is separate from the other, yet both together take a single look. One ear is separate from the other, yet they vibrate to the same sound. One hand is separate from the other, yet they match in gesture. One leg is separate from the other, yet together they allow us to walk.

Who could ever say which distance separates word from mouth, or from the loving fingers copying it? And a man from the man repeating him? And the universe from the universe embracing it?

And what, finally, is this non-distance that postures as distance only to abolish it?

All splits off from All to allow us to conceive of the All, which otherwise would be unthinkable. Nothing is separate from Nothing so that they might mirror each other and thus be named by Nothing.

Does life, does a work take shape in the interval between Nothing and Nothing? Come out of Nothing, out of All turned into Nothing only to sink back into the nothingness of All? Our projects and desires corroborate it. Stones are dust. An entire life is in a breath: a bit of oxygen pilfered from the air. Life depends on a heartbeat, and the world on a blinking eyelid. In the stream of life, book follows book.

Very far then, here where distance takes refuge.

(*In the words* ÉLOIGNEMENT, LOINTAIN, *"distance," "remoteness," there is the word* LOI, *"law,"
as also in the word* OEIL, *"eye," as quoted above.*

*Is it not strange, by the way, that we use "above"
to refer a reader to a quotation already written when
I should really write "below" since we speak of "con-
structing a work," and the only way to build is from
the bottom up. But we read pages from top to bottom.
Which shows that the top is sometimes the bottom
and vice versa. With this settled, let us go back to the
text, which we never, in any case, left.*

*The law is in the eye. Distance is the field of the
eye, the extent of its law. The law it submits to and
imposes. The eye fashions the law, which fashioned
it. It will be extinguished with the last manifestation
of this implacable law, along with all that dies of its
intransigence.*

The word LOI, *"law," is also in the words* PLOIE,
DÉPLOIE, EMPLOIE, *"bend," "display," "employ." It
governs what is employed or displayed, all that at
some time or other bends under the rigor of the law.
Texts are subject to law. Some words tell us so: rash,
garrulous words, which, before even saying themselves, cry "Law." With the final word, the law of the
text surfaces from the heart of its practice—but did
we not intuitively follow its tracks all along?—Likewise the presentiment of living an exceptional morning, which exalts the writer glued to his pen all
through the night of the word, can only be confirmed
at dawn, with the appearance of Sun-Law, the word*
SOLEIL, *which contains, how could we doubt it, the
words* OEIL *and* LOI *in mysterious order, gigantic
pupil, heavenly eye with lashes of fire.*

*Did not Reb Ayoub write: "Our laws are in the
sun. Their light floods the universe"?*

*And Reb Gab: "Clear limpidity of the law. God
sees"?)*

The law is always in the background. It is protected by distance. It owes its power and prestige to its perspective. It is elsewhere in relation to here, but it is an elsewhere-within, as if its measure and menace. So that being here means submitting to the law of growing remoteness whose here is but the undefined place where it holds sway. Here is never local. It can spread over the whole world. Hence being here means being wherever this here is given as *here*, means acknowledging its dependence on the law that temporarily stabilizes it and weighs on it with all the weight of its alienated space.

The law creates a *here* of the law, which is accepted only in our eventual recognition of the law. Hence we are master of the here, alone to call it so. But if the here of the law, the place where it proclaims and imprints itself, were the book? In that case, the book would be both its here and elsewhere. It would be the incommensurate space of the law in its written form, the very space of its writing, giddy with its foundation, mixing the application of here and elsewhere—the elsewhere no longer quite showing as elsewhere, or the here as totally here. We are under the yoke of the law as we are subject to the infinite and the indefinitely finite, to the habitable and uninhabitable, to eternity and the moment.— The book would finally, we might say, be *the here of the elsewhere that rescinds it,* the void of here and the here of the void. For the law of the book is a law of abysses, and the book transmitting it, the abyss of the law.

If the chief aim of writing were simply to teach us to read the law, without which there can be no writing, then all writing would be a reading of the law that rules it as it rules the universe, a law we violate under penalty of being cut off from the book.

(Taking our distance is not absence. On the contrary. Assessing the space that separates us from an object, a place, a sorb-apple, restores them to their true dimension.

Could it be that God's absence is only due to His

*taking His distance? Farther than the farthest? The
mind can conceive of this, and the believer's heart
suffer even though reassured in his belief.*
    *—But God is without dimension. He is the measure
of All.*

    *"God is the distance of the Law and, through the
Law, present everywhere," he said to me.*

    *"God," I said to myself, "is perhaps only the dis-
tance that separates us from any idea of God: the
solitude of an idea.")*

III

Digression is the lonely man's course par excellence. But could
we not, by taking some other route, get to the end of our solitude?
Tomorrow is tied to all the days-after champing at the bit. This race
is without mercy, that is to say, without pity or thanks. Tomorrow
blazes above thousands of exhausted horses.

Yesterday is our solitude and so is tomorrow. If man is made in
God's image he must, like Him, be eternally alone. Every book is
a book of solitude, of an absence from the world that the world
inhabits and the word ushers in.

*

I was born on April 16 . . . If I come back to this sentence in its
third phase, it is to present the following. Although in fact born on
April 16, I could claim only the date of the 14th marked in my
passport. The triumphant lie—though nobody lied—supplants the
truth it has reduced to silence. The false birth date officially recorded wipes out the true one. On the 14th, I was still moving in
my mother's womb. A warm, red night enveloped me, filled my
eyes. I prepared to face my birth as if I were going to be born of
myself. Little by little, I wrested from the void the face that became

mine. I was a weak creature living the last hours of before-life, a creature without name gloomily waiting for one, a creature outside language, an embryo of a letter, a word. Ah, was I really born in Cairo, at the dawn of this 16th of April when my mother gave birth to me? My first scream certainly came at that moment, spattered with blood, and remained engraved in her memory. If being born is simply coming into the world, then I was born on April 16 around 4:00 AM, according to my mother. But do we not come into the world as we go to our death, in sacrificial innocence? As if death opened our eyes onto itself?

"There are eyes behind our eyes," said a sage, "that see as the seed sees before the flower, and will still see when our eyes have wilted. Life, death are one and the same persistent glance."

At the beginning of the first *Book of Questions*, one of the characters says:

"When, as a child, I wrote my name for the first time, I knew I was beginning a book."

If we admit that we exist only in and through our name, that naming gives existence to the named being or thing, allows it to appear and assert itself as a specific being or thing; if we realize also that nothing exists outside the book, that the universe is in the book, that is, it is the book through which, through each of whose pages, it becomes the universe; if, moreover, we cannot ignore the writer's experience that, having a name, we are nothing more for the book than the letters that form this word we have become, and that this word is fully realized only in the sentence, the moment shared with the book, where it gets its true dimension among the words it defies or makes pacts with, then we may claim we were born on the day we entered the book, the moment we began being written by it. But a book is always the beginning of the incomplete book defined by its very incompleteness, the beginning of an interrupted rebeginning whose sense and key lie in the hands of death. Remains to be seen what the book is and what was the book of our very first childhood. An erased book, no doubt, whose erasure is remembered by all books.

No sooner do we enter the book than we are no longer the same. But is this not so with every risk we take, even in the most common

situations? Being part of the world, defining ourselves, means suddenly becoming another person: *the other*, who awaited or dreaded
his hour—an hour that includes his strung-out hours of waiting and
apprehension. It is true that whole days, months, years can come
to a head in a few fateful minutes. So a word, a gesture is enough
to turn us into another: our double tied to surprise or anxiety,
revolt, desire, fear, to the wonder shaped by death.

Then writing would be only a particular kind of action, all the
more dangerous for taking place entirely inside ourselves. For us,
to be sure, but also against us, with the studied design of killing us
for the benefit of another—ourselves?—born of our hope or misery
and who claims our name.

Could the book of our first infancy be the forebook of which we
die? Could it be the book of death we leaf through alongside our
books, without ever knowing for sure if it is our companion and
"the book within the book"?

Then being named would mean accepting the destiny of life from
the hands of death, would mean that the named person rises out of
the dark toward day; a day itself within the day, older than that of
our birth, whose arrival we mark with the feverish slant of a sig-
nature. Nothing, however, comes to pass but has been long and
carefully prepared as if outside ourselves, which might make us
think that this "outside" is the rock bottom. For the body written
has, like the book, no limits and might lead us to think that it is
writing that explodes limitations, *that there is no unlimited experience outside writing*, which, having unquestioned power to de-
limit, assigns new frontiers, which will in turn be overrun someday.
The infinite, like a spotless page, is spattered with invisible frontiers, which the human mind in its weakness has imposed on the
word, and which the word in turn imposes on the mind to force it
to reject them and no longer rest in peace.

But if there is only the beginning of a book, then there is never
any book. And how can we know if we are in the book if the book
is but its own absence revealed by words, is but the book of an
absence it maintains fictitiously through go-between words of an
elsewhere judged accessible, on which absence would break, spell-
bound. An elsewhere itself thrown to words as if to the dogs, torn

to pieces, which we gather up on and around the corpse of the Word. Do we know this (albeit without understanding clearly) because we are ourselves the breath of an absence, whose rhythm our body takes on and to whose ambiguity we add our name? The presence of an absence in sham projection that our gestures extend beyond their domain, and as if this extension defined their reach. Absence more than real from which our actions draw their relative assurance and their necessity.

To know that we are in the book means we have become convinced that its absence is ours. We are always at the threshold of an intolerable absence about to declare itself, and which stifles the vocables that crowd around as if their future depended on this very same absence, from one definite point of space it occupies (and which their past denounces) to the infinite of the other. For word and world, like ourselves, are perpetually becoming, and, hence, an absence that only wants to wed its image. And is the image not always ahead?

We must not think that absence lacks images. Without them we could not conceive of absence. Images of images rejected by almighty presence and which, O irony, propagate it. Thus our lightest step encounters tracks our heels could have left on the ground, nonexistent tracks, but which alone could account for our multiple passages. Tracks in the void, where absence gets lost at the borders of the unsuspected, as the blue of sky at the horizon.

The absent book calls out for vocables. The book's voice is toneless, a silent voice that speaks only to the eye, at the heart of the law. This call gives away its presence somewhere.—Vocable: *vocabulum*, from *vocare* = to call. Does the book transform into vocables the called words that, impatient to join it, also called the book, are still calling it? Desire fed by the desire it kindles, desire of a desire fanned by its own echo?

So the absent book is perhaps only the indefinite space of the book's desire for vocabulary and the vocables' desire for the book. Desire to write, which writing will maintain with desire, having made it the reason for all writing. For the sky is sky only to be written in words of desire for sky. For the earth is earth only to be written in words of desire for earth. For man is man only to be written in the insatiable words of his desire: the very same words. The law of the book is the law of desire.

The abyss of desire is the fathomless depth of the law, vertigo of the pact.

The past is not death, but death's chance to change a certain future—its own? ours?—into fictional time where our history, once exhumed, can be rewritten at the pleasure of our pen. Immense story, which has conquered oblivion, but which oblivion had already confronted with excess: excess, itself at the origin of the creation it makes burst forth.

In this sense, the past of all writing sees itself as a memory of death, memory of the void that keeps it from dying. Thus there is a past sunk inside the words' own past, through which death operates. For there can be no language outside death. Creation killed God, who has ever since lived only the life of His Creation, never His own given life, but a life received.

The book is the place of the neutral whose neutrality is always endangered, a place where two equally strong forces are opposed in a fight without respite, but also without conclusion. As they keep close watch on each other, any lapse on either side could be only temporary. The losing force would immediately double its efforts and reestablish the momentarily imperiled balance.

On one side, writing: what is done, what is written in the book. On the other, facing it, non-writing: what is undone and erased in the book. And as if the erasure were writing in order to be erased.

The neutrality of the book is matched by the writer's.

And what is questioning but waking these supremely active forces, which an answer will paralyze and then revive, what is it but the neutral rising out of its refuted negation, of which death is the expression that never runs dry—death, in which creative life and destructive life wrestle each other with indomitable fire, with their original, indivisible truth?

The neutrality of book and death lies in the name they escape, which, left to itself, has become the name of their absence.

God's life outside the Name is the life of a humble word, life of
a life out of His reach, which at the darkest point of the unnamable
names Him in all His banality.

(NOM, *"name," should be read twice, from left to
right and from right to left, because two words com-
pose it:* NOM *and* MON, *my name. This name is mine.
All names are personal.*

*"God is the impersonality of a name, the univer-
sality of all words of existence," wrote Reb Azrel.*

*"This is obvious," replied Reb Amlak. "But your
reflection, Master, leads me to ask: What is a word
that nobody claims, that no object demands? What is
a word without referent, without respondent?*

*"What are, in an absolute sense, those words that
transport and destroy us, like: Truth; Freedom; Love;
Death? Signs desperate for being neither recognized
nor heard.*

*"Words that are not taken in are lost. And we have
no doubt created them the better to live our loss.*

*"A word exists only through and for us, who are
nothing, and the object it designates, which is dust.*

*"Ah, in this nothing, in this grey powder of time,
there tremble the pinioned wings of eternity ready
for flight."*

*And Reb Allam: "I write. I am all the words born
of me in order to hurl me into the void. As if the act
of writing were at the same time intoxication with life
and mad passion for death."*

*In God, Evil and Good, Lie and Truth, Dark and
Light, Water and Fire, Word and Silence, Thought
and the Unthought cancel each other out to Nothing,
where the enclosed word* NO *causes trouble. For
Nothing became nothing by saying No to everything;
but what does it become by saying No to itself?*

God is the chance of Nothing.

God is perhaps only the chance of those two letters
which, within the word NOTHING, *say* NO *to this*
word.)

IV

I was born on April 16. In this fourth phase of my questioning,
I should perhaps leave it to my body to confirm or deny, after day
and hour, the year of my birth. Only the body knows its age. And
our age would be simply that of our body if it were not for thought,
which, in opening the book to steer it to its final word, also opens
the universe of a day to be stripped to its last glimmer.

No matter what I undertake or construct, no matter how far I
advance in the steps of thinking, my lifetime will never be more
than that of my body. As if the body in its unlimited closure were
the readable limit of the book.

All we are able to feel, understand, contemplate: this world that
subjects us, this half-tamed infinite where words get lost, giddy
with their loss because they can reach us only across their silent
vanishing—all the things that capture, release, carry, destroy us
are bound to the body and the space it bestows, to the body, which
alone holds their future.

Without body we would have no world. Hearing, sight, smell
signal it to our mind, which questions it for them.

Without body we would be a breath in the wind, a silence within
silence. Without body there would be no book. As if absence of
books were but suppression of the body.

But could we, without body, even tell presence from absence,
waking from sleep, dawn from dusk? And what is a breath for the
wind, a silence for silence, when it is the body that speaks or is
quiet, breathes or expires; when it is the body that names and
comes to terms with each name? And what is the book except the
body's long preparation for the hidden words of its absence?

Is the age of the body the age of the text? If I write a text in three days, can I say the text is three days old? This would also mean that the age of the book containing this text would correspond to the sum of hours of its pages. Now we know that the pages of a book are not added up, but cut. From the book's innumerable immaculate pages we pull out those that we cover with words. To fill them all is unimaginable. Numbering the pages of a book means numbering the pages we took out of the book. Each one refers to a virgin page.

Multitudinous body, justified. Do we owe it to the vocabulary of our five senses that we have a body ready to give body—its own— to all that seeks existence: a vegetal, animal or human body, body of a scent, a sound, a presence or absence? All along the book, death scatters our bodies pell-mell. There will always be a body that makes us die its death.

The dejection, even prostration, that usually precedes the act of writing or follows upon it—what can we trace it to unless perhaps to the body's failure to mount resistance against a death that a priori would bear only on its eyes or mind, on the work of its hand? Momentary failure from which the body recovers quickly, so strong is its vitality, so unquenched its thirst for the unknown.

To die through language a death other than our own (to which our own death finally submits) and to survive this death that abandons us to its void—does this not mean realizing that we are ourselves creatures of the void words pledge us to?

If my body bred the precarious bodies I inhabit, then it must be the oldest of them all. And the lives of all those bodies will never go beyond that of my flesh and bones, my life, what I feel the right to call my life although I do not know at which moment it began or will end, as if, though it be mine, I were in no way its beneficiary.

So why make to-do about a birth date? Saying "I was born on . . ." is as absurd as declaring "I shall die on . . ." because there are no frontiers between life and death, and because the body that has felt this entanglement knows it will die of it. Being born is already suicide.

I used to think that writing leads to suicide. I was wrong. Death uses writing to tempt us. Eyes bandaged as in a game of blindman's buff, we play at recognizing it: Death, the condemned word that reduces its own letters to ashes.

*

If all the books within the book must keep within the number of its pages, our multiple, successive lives cannot have any duration apart from the unique, unpredictable life of a body.

The body opens like a book, and the word, pushed by thought, rushes out to conquer the unknown. But the unthought will be its death.

If we do not die of our words it is no doubt because they carry our thoughts, and we are incapable of thinking the unthought.

The future of flesh can only be flesh.

The time of the book is perhaps only the time, conjugated in all modes, of an unsayable birth.

And the story, the surprising burst of a word.

("The passage from life to death is never brought about without blows and difficulties.

"Passage of reciprocal powers.

"How come it hardly affects me today?" wrote Reb Allouan.

Approach thought through the slant of your thinking, the word through your go-between words, life through the channel of your life, death through the detour of your death.

Thus you will appreciate them from the inside and become familiar with their mechanisms.

In the same way, you can approach the book through the book, through its deep ambitions, and adjust the rhythm of your breathing to its breath.

Every wager is first of all a wager with yourself.

You have to open the casing of a watch to enter into time's secret.

Never be late or early for a word.

"*Every thought lives on in the thought that super-sedes it, as dimly perceived origin. Never the first origin, but the last, which is, however, considered the origin whose revelation reveals all the others from which it issued, even to the one vanished before be-fore-the-origin.*

"*Is there such a thing as a first thought? A last thought?*

"*Thought is. God is, by virtue of being universal thought, all the thoughts contained in Thinking.*

"*We cannot think except in God,*" *he said.*

"*Is it not surprising that God, who does not write, should be He who writes, and that man, who writes incessantly, never writes anything?*

"*We read God in the white spaces of our texts, just as we discover the sun's dazzling, lyrical pages in the dense and mute dark of night,*" *noted Reb Tabah.*

And added: "*Imagine invisible rows of books to the infinite.*

"*Then you realize on what a fragile foundation the sky rests. And what rival thoughts fissure it each day.*"

"*The air is written. We breathe words. Writing means perhaps reproducing the words of our breath in their regained appearance,*" *he said.*

Dust, dust of our eternal Bibles.
God is mortal for being a word.)

*

Once written, the book is virgin of readings.

As if nothing had been read but was written for oblivion. As if every word were set in oblivion so that it could be read.

Posthumous virginity.

ON HUMOR

"A fact harmless in itself may sometimes be at the origin of considerable events.

"We never notice right away. This is my first lesson.

"As for the second: There is no human discovery that is not mostly a profound manifestation of divine humor," wrote Reb Gazi.

And Reb Bittar: "What a sense of humor: God hides us from ourselves so that one day our most natural gestures may astonish us."

"The greatest of our learned men were humorists," said Reb Botton. And added: "Living in a state of sanctity may mean pushing humor all the way to its negation, which is another form of humor."

"All choice is humorous. All creation, a wager of humor," wrote Reb Aris.

"Give me an example of God's humor."
"Man."
"Give me an example of man's humor."
"God," wrote Reb Nassif.

" 'The first mark in space was a mark of humor. What will be the last, the cruelest?' asked Reb Amhat of Reb Zahar.

" 'Perhaps,' the latter replied, 'an invisible point.'

"And he told the story of a man who one night talked so long with God that his face kept to his death the same malicious smile, a reflection of his infinite knowledge," reported Reb Assoud.

"All these tears, no doubt to slake our thirst for humor . . ." Reb Aris wrote also.

WHOSE SEAL CANNOT BE BROKEN

"If I were to speak of death, I would say: My father and mother are dead, likewise my brother and sister. Many of my friends are dead. It seems this ought to be enough."

"It might be enough, all right, but is speaking of death the same thing as evoking one's dead? If I may refer to your books . . ."

"If I were to speak of death with reference to my books, I would say: Sarah and Yukel are dead, also Yaël and Elya. It seems this ought to be enough."

"It might be enough, all right, but what have all these deaths to do with yours?"

"I died with my father and mother. I died with Sarah and Yukel, with Yaël and her stillborn child. I died with all those I have seen die, died their death. I died with the countless characters peopling my books, even if I remember only their voices, even if I wrote only a few of their words in my notebook.

"Ah, how many times have I died with myself?"

"Then speaking of death is the same thing as evoking one's dead?"

"Of death we can speak only to death; we speak of it for its sake alone."

"Yet we are speaking of ourselves."

"Death cuts us short, takes back the words it had lent us for a while.

"Dying means letting go of our words against our will. We speak only for the sake of death until it prefers silence."

"Could silence be another form of speech?"

". . . perhaps speech without speech like a day without day, a trace without trace."

". . . an appeal without appeal, a farewell without farewell?"

". . . perhaps like a hole in the void, the free emptiness of a hole."

(Death is an indestructible tie. More so than blood and love. Dare I write: the only tie?

"There could be no ties without death," said Reb Chohet, "because without death there is no time, and ties are but time's desire forged into the time that breaks it."

And he added: "What ties time to eternity is no other than death, which both limits and dissolves.

"Ties are inscribed in the imperiled perpetuity of day pursued by night.

"Eternity is then only the infinite desire of time sacrificed to its own desire, the coveted, desirable second.")

BORN VIABLE

It is with thought as with a newborn infant.
Viable or not.
Likewise with the book.

"The total book is the most vulnerable. O vulnerability of God!"
Reb Abravanel had written.

And had added: "The eternal book is not one where page after page would display the sum of human knowledge—for what is more short-lived than knowledge?—but, on the contrary, the book destroyed by the book it engenders, which will in turn be destroyed.

"Its eternity is in the renewed sacrifice of its resemblance."

Here, thought could not follow me. What is this absence of thought that is not given as absent, but as the thought of an absence of thought?

—Or perhaps absence as thought by its absence, death as thought by death. It is this thought, over which thinking has no hold, that we approach momentarily at the edge of silence.

Thus we die of a thought that was never ours, but was all through our life the thought that would have thought us from the moment of our birth.

Not to think anymore. To be the thought of the universe. To drown in it, O void, O nothingness!

And yet I think myself outside my thoughts, even outside the thought that thinks me, but like the air for which I am space, like the ocean for which I am wave, like the log in the fire, for which I am ashes, burning ashes . . .

"We shall be led through our night by a thought that our thinking will not lose sight of."

"Then time is only a thought of time, which man tried to adapt to his limits. A time thought within the thinking of time."

If tomorrow has already been thought, is the future not simply a thought that opens the road for the thinking we undertake?

God cannot be thought. Being Thought of the future He always remains to be thought.

*

Here, already, is your chance to approach the place. With every movement you displace a frontier. Nothing can be bounded forever. You elude the traps. Unless the trap is the universe. You lift an arm and violate a new space. You turn your head or risk a step forward and are no longer in the same infinite.

It is then the desert speaks, and its speech is inaudible because too vast. It is then you try to speak for the desert, but your words do not carry. They are undone as soon as you pronounce them in your mind. Your mouth is all sand; your eye, all emptiness. There are no borders except inside you. They are lines of silence along which thought, like a tightrope walker, fears, at the slightest lapse, to tumble into the void.

. . . it is this threatened thought that guides us from book to book, from wager to wager . . .

God luxuriates in the vulnerability of this thought.

> *(The body of Thought stiffens at the sight of death.*
>
> *. . . a death it will not have had leisure to think.)*

THOUGHT, DEATH

Death turns into thought only to try to think itself
one last time at the invincible height—or depth—
where all thinking abdicates.
For no thought is susceptible of thinking death.
Only death itself might perhaps be capable of it.
O ashes fed by ashes.

Does thought have a passion? And what could it be
except perhaps a thought of love whose thinking we
would embrace?

"We should never speak of death," said an old rabbi on his death-
bed, "because we cannot speak of what we do not know. Nothingness is unthinkable."
So conceiving of death would only mean conceiving ourselves
dead. And that would lead only to arbitrary and unverifiable hy-
potheses. Yet we live with death.
Can we speak of life? In that case we should be able to speak
of death as a subterranean life, a life underneath life animated
by death, a life that would allow death to die, to be its own
death.
We live with death as with a strange woman whose doings we
dread, whose thoughts we sometimes guess. At best we anticipate
her reactions, yet without knowing anything about her projects,
neither who she is nor where she came from, nor at what moment

we knew for certain that she has always been with us and will go with us to the grave.

("Death; the life that kills."
Reb Hazan.)

ON BLANKNESS, I

1

No face but responds to a hand's desire. No hand but is haunted by a face.

My books bear witness to a practice of text tied to an experience of which I could not say to what point it is the experience of all words—so inseparable, so solidary are they in the face of risk.

"I was born in the book. I grew up in the book. I shall die in the book. I have known no other home, no other roads, no other landscape or sky," he said.

And added: "I have never lifted my eyes from the book."

Did not Reb Saadia write: "I was born with the book as we are born with a shadow. At night, my book and I are one"?

2

When a writer thinks he has come out of his solitude he is most alone.

I read and reread the last book I am going to write.

. . . I am read and reread by my last book, which is but my next book ambitious to be unique.

The infinite of the book is the vital space of the vocable, its death.

3

"The truth of the book we might perhaps find beyond words, where the vocable is without hope, on the horizon of all objections pleaded."

He remembers these words of Reb Aron's, who died ten centuries ago: "   ," and says to himself that with this one sentence he could have made a book.

He remembers these words of Reb Maimoun's, who died seven centuries ago: "   ," and says to himself that with this one sentence he could have made a book.

He remembers these words of Reb Zirah's, who died three centuries ago: "   ," and says to himself that with this one sentence he could have made a book.

He remembers these words of Reb Zibri's, who died one century ago: "   ," and says to himself that with this one sentence he could have made a book.

He remembers these words of Reb Benayoun's, who just died: "   ," and says to himself that with this one sentence he could have made a book.

("What are these sentences you refer to," he was
asked, "of which only the quotation marks remain?"
    "Sentences erased along with the book that you can
now read only in its intractable blankness, that of the
page."

    "So blank do our books become one day that we
doubt we wrote them," Reb Gabri had noted.

    Quotation marks are marks our nails have scratched
on the wall of our misery. Our walls were books. Did
not Reb Mosri say: "O that your forehead, eyes, and
hands would merge into the wall. Then you could
read God's petrified words that can only be deci-
phered from inside. And you would find the words of
our old books with their wholesome freshness. Your
tears would momentarily restore the original color to
their letters faded over the centuries.")

It was rainy that morning, fall weather. The question had turned
away from man, had crumbled the book. It had allowed itself to
waste away like those bedridden old men who one day stop eating
and, in their weak state, look out their windows at nothing but
emptiness.
    Nothing in this landscape but dense clouds and, all across, ob-
sessive birds in low flight, whirling words nobody cares about.

    (They secretly passed the book around, and every-
body read his own history in it, as one reads the
absence of stars in a winter sky.)

ON BLANKNESS, II

"The Name of God is a blank, the Messiah's nearly as much so," he said.

"The Messiah will reveal himself. The letters of his name will be visible as blank," he also said.

"My son came to me out of his name," said Yaël. "I have lived the name of my son."

"What name could a stillborn child claim?" she was asked.

"The name I shall choose for him," she had replied. "*Aely* or *Elya*. I hesitate between these two.

"The name I shall choose for my son will be the Messiah's."

"The Messiah's name is in every name," she was told with a touch of irony.

"My son will come to me through his name," Yaël had said, "and I shall be reborn through him.

"Elya will be the Messiah's name.

"Tarnished blank of Elya, pure blank of Aely."

ON BLANKNESS, III

"Blank is our solitude at its end," said Reb Zakar.
"God covers it with His own, as an unfolded shroud
would cover a smaller shroud."

"From white to white, how many intermediary colors, which we can only perceive by comparison! How
many disappointing incursions into transitory whiteness!
"Whiteness comes always *after* white," wrote Reb
Hassoud.

"I who am separated from you by all that unites us, separated by
the same space and the same transparency of words, I know that
exile is an apprenticeship in blankness and that therefore a blank
can never be a different blank because there cannot be twin uni-
verses," said Reb Saffouan.
"Except in death," replied Reb Hames, "where all is blank for
no longer being."

("*The foretold time of times would only be an arc
of becoming, the curve of the horizon where you
evolve,*" Reb Ségré had written.
"*. . . the curve of the horizon where you are no
more,*" emended later his disciple, Reb Sullam. "*Because the Time of times is only shards of a time become ours, as the time of God is a consummate break
with the ledger time of man.*")

THE LOST BOOK

"Read us the book again."

"I have been careless and lost it."

"A peddler once offered my grandfather a unique book. I have inherited it. It is perhaps yours?"

"Open it. And we will see."

"There's not a word written."

"My grandfather once brought back a book from a trip to the Orient. Here it is. It is perhaps yours?"

"Open it. And we will see."

"There's not a word written."

"My old uncle gave me, shortly before his death, a book he had vainly tried to decipher. I have it in my hands. It is perhaps yours?"

"Open it. And we will see."

"There's not a word written."

"A friend sent me for my birthday a strange book from the distant country he is from. I have it in my pocket. It is perhaps yours?"

"Open it. And we will see."

"There's not a word written."

"One afternoon I found a book on a park bench. It's under my arm. It is perhaps yours?"

"Open it. And we will see."

"There's not a word written."

"One morning I woke with my head between the pages of an

untitled book, which I had, more fascinated than intrigued, leafed through in my dream. I brought it for you. It is perhaps yours?"
"Open it. And we will see."
"There's not a word written."

"My neighbor just returned this book I had lent him a long time ago and which a knowledgeable collector had judged more profound than the abyss. I'm giving it to you. It is perhaps yours?"
"Open it. And we will see."
"There's not a word written."
"Have I written a book?"
"Did you not read us passages from it?"
"I have indeed read you some pages of the book."
"Of which book?"
"A found book."
"Each of us has given you a book."
"I have indeed read extracts from all of them."
". . . but nothing was written there."
"Then perhaps it was my book after all."

"With all these blanks we shall, after the example of God, form a blank word to read through His eyes only," Reb Assaf had written.
And Reb Farhi: "Will Your eyes, O Lord, someday guide my eyes in their reading?
"Then I could finally read Your Book within mine."

"I am only the poor body of a man," wrote Reb Ishak, "with eyes of God."
And he added: "Is not the iris the particle of God that openly, in the sight of all, binds us to the universe?"

In every beginning, God sees the end, and in every end, the new beginning.
O Desert, vigilance of sand.

"The soul is the awakening of the eye. My body will snuff out my soul before it perishes; but for a brief moment, my room will be bathed in a dim light as of a candle that our eyes still see after it has been blown out.

"This pale glimmer is perhaps eternal. Death mistakes it for daylight," Reb Alam had written.

And Reb Sadoun: "There is a light stolen from the dark, the blue light of the soul best vouched for by the blind.

"Night is overcome."

". . . this infinite, pale glimmer, O victory of our immortal eyes," he said.

HERE, THE END

Here, the end of words, of the book, of chance.

Desert.
Throw the die. It will desert you.

Here, the end of the game, of resemblance.
The infinite, with the help of its letters, denies the end.

Here, the end cannot be denied. It is infinite.

Here, no place,
not even a vestige.

Here, only sand.

The Desert

"The word of our origin is a word of the desert, O desert of our words," wrote Reb Aslan.

"There is no place for the man whose steps head toward his place of birth;
"as if being born meant only walking toward your birth.
"My future, my origin," he said.

"There is no possible return if you have gone deep into the desert. Come from elsewhere, the elsewhere is your twin horizon.
"Sand, the asking. Sand, the reply. Our desert has no limits," wrote Reb Semama.

He held a bit of sand in each hand: "On the one hand, questions, on the other, answers. Same weight of dust," he also said.

To create means to make the future the past of all your actions.

With exemplary regularity the Jew chooses to set out for the desert, to go toward a renewed word that has become his origin.

"In creating, you create the origin that swallows you," wrote Reb Sanua.

"The origin is an abyss."

Reb Behit.

*

"If God spoke in the desert, it was to deprive His word of roots, so that the creature should be His privileged bond. We shall make our souls into a hidden oasis," said Reb Abravanel.

"And of His written word," asked his disciple, "what shall we make of that?"

"Of his fiery vocables we shall make a book of inconsumable fire," replied Reb Abravanel.

But Reb Hassoud, whose bold statements and commentaries were most often badly received by the interpreters, spoke up:

"A wandering word is the word of God. It has for echo the word of a wandering people. No oasis for it, no shadow, no peace. Only the immense, thirsty desert, only the book of this thirst, the devastating fire of this fire reducing all books to ashes at the threshold of the obsessive, illegible Book bequeathed us."

"What have we done other than forever call ourselves into question by examining everything down to the buzzing fly? Here is our humble merit and the source of our despair," wrote Reb Feroush.

"At which moment of painful impotence must we impose on the book an end to our reading?

"I close my eyes. I refuse to go on.

"Let the book come finally free of our chains," he had noted.

PREY TO THE DESERT WIND

The man who was found lying in his blood near the old caravan trail had usurped my name.

"Every time you use the pronoun *Je*, "I," you name me, because my last name begins with *J*, and my first with *E*," he once wrote me.

In this way he who was *I* entered my books, in my place.

Ah, let the sand cover him.

The dunes are perhaps the dust of a million graves, our true beds for eternity, safe from the indiscreet.

At this point, my concierge came up and pointed at the body:

"This man was one of the people in our building. I recognize him. He is a writer. He once threw himself out of his fourth-floor window. His suicide, from what I've heard, is written up in the seventh volume of *The Book of Questions*. You can look it up. But how did he manage to revive and come to die in this desert? And me too, by what miracle did I get here with you people?

"I have a feeling I am a different woman, my spitting image.

"Bah, if all the dead end up the same, why shouldn't the living?

"You may object that these are the ideas of a concierge. But like everybody I must reason in my own way and think as I can, right?

"I admit these events are beyond my understanding."

"Look how death outlines distant horizons," Sarah had written to Yukel. "All these well-defined spaces are ours."

"An acre of fertile soil for life. A patch in the void for death.

"Insular like life, is death," he said.

They had lived on an island, a small island. Around them, no sea, no ocean. Around them, no water. Just enough air to breathe.

An island their own, for their clasped bodies, their rebellious souls.

Neither garden nor house nor room.

Neither stars nor trees nor sun nor torrents,

only walls

high, so high

that the night inside

rising up against all night

was not seen by the universe.

"We were this inner, this protected night, Sarah," Yukel had written.

How is it possible that the writer whose body we have just discovered could have died twice—both times, it seems, in equally tragic and inexplicable circumstances? First in the Western city he lived in, then in the Orient, amid sand?

No mystery underneath, but the irresistible call of the abyss heard even on the other side of death.

"We enter, all innocence, into the dream of death and cannot imagine to what dangers we expose ourselves," Reb Mazliah had written.

"One day the wind with all its breath will sweep the sky clean, and the desert will finally mirror the desert," he had noted.

"Who will ever denounce the awesome ambition of dream, this

uncontrollable force of the dark regions for which we are miserable
toys?" he had also written.

> "Beautiful stranger,
> dew is your face;
> dream, your hair;
> the dark, your sex;
> morning, your ankles.
> Give a drink to the well
> that has lost its mind,"

sang Sarah, prey to her delirious mind, in her white prison at the
borders of the unknowable, before she turned into a mortally
bruised desert where the winds came crashing down.

"Before and after the name, there is the desert," wrote Reb
Hamza.

And he added: "What is the desert other than the dissolved past
before our own past, as well as our solidary future?"

In the desert, fire is a mockery.

BEFORE THE DESERT

"When a sob is but a song, when a song is but a name, then the Messiah will come," said Reb Ayache.

There is no name that is not a desert. There is no desert but was once a name.

He claimed "the Jews were the suffering part of humanity after having been its happy part."
He said that "every writer was heir to both parts.
"One part of pain against one part of joy." Likewise our books.

"Mad as fire, with a craze to consume," he had also said.
And elsewhere: "For what have I struggled as desperately as to have a name?"
Did not Reb Béhit write: "Every disciple loses his name, keeps only the name of his teacher"?
And farther on: "I have God for a disciple. Has He, my favorite student, made my name His?"

The old silver watch that Reb Foueka always carried on a chain of the same metal hit one corner of his desk so violently that it half spilled at his feet while the other half dangled in the air by the chair he was sitting in, between armrest and floor.
Reb Foueka bent down and gathered up the shell with broken crystal, hands, and dial.
"The mechanism seems intact," he mumbled to himself, putting

everything in his drawer. "Rayad, the watchmaker, will surely be able to fix it."

Afterward he said to himself that he was perhaps wrong to be concerned with time; that it was mad to think we could assign a time to truth or love; that all thought, all belief, all feeling could only spread over the days and sometimes years they flooded; that measured time was only an aid to memory, and at the end of forgetting, God reigned in His inaugural absence.

He put out his lamp because it was late.

"In the dark, nobody needs a watch," he went on mumbling. "The dark is our universe. From birth to death, every letter of our books confronts us with the same night."

He woke up in the wee hours of the morning having crossed eternity unawares.

AFTER THE DESERT

Fire teams up with riches or misery, with leaves or grain, with a star or a pebble.
The desert frightens the fire.

"The Word of God, which is of fire, was short-lived and localized because the desert kept it from spreading. But how come it still resonates in the universe as the very cry of life? That is because the desert rejected it," wrote Reb Basri.

"And, struck by El's lightning, the universe will in the end lie down on the desert, golden dust on golden sand, for an everlasting sleep.
"Thus we learned by instinct that God was death," Reb Assayas had written.
And elsewhere: "Ah, do not trust this divine Word of life, because it comes out of the black gullet of death. And it is your death it speaks to.
"While you are alive you can have only the vaguest inkling of the Word of God."

"I hear the distant voice of God," said Reb Toueta. "I enter, passive, into death."

All these heads without necks.
All these necks without shoulders.
All these shoulders without torsos.
All these torsos without lungs.

All these lungs without bellies.
All these bellies without hips.
All these hips without legs.
All these legs without feet.
All these feet without ground.
All these books without titles.
All these titles without pages.
All these pages without sentences.
All these sentences without words.
All these words without letters.
All these letters without ink.
All this ink without night.
All these nights without sleep.
. . . this sleep without waking.
. . . this waking without sun.

And Reb Ayad said: "What is the desert but a test of complete-
ness, a death within daily death?"

And Yukel said: "Solitude of our fallen heads, our undone shoulders. Solitude of our crushed torsos and lungs. Solitude of our broken hips, our paralyzed legs. Solitude of our mornings and nights,
of our eyes without face and hands without arms, our tongue and
our books.

"O Sarah, does a body in pieces know it once was a body? Does
it aspire to reunite its scattered parts? What means could it invent
to this end? Which of its parts would have sufficient strength to
take the initiative?

"Unity is only an ardent desire for union, and totality, only chosen fragments prone to break.

"Only the desert—maybe because this afterworld is like an un-
discovered cancer in the full body of the universe, the ineluctable
end of all ends of a renascent but doomed world—was and could
not but be, against the sky, the celestial void—as we are all against
the light that returns us to our shadow, against the night that returns us to dawn—was and could not but be, from one horizon to
the next, our supreme bond with death."

"What is more insolent than death?" asked Reb Eliaram of his teacher, Reb Saada.

"Perhaps after-death, the brazen future of our much feared absence," the latter replied.

"The desert is always vastness recovered from our deserts.

"O death after death.

"O fire before the flame.

"The desert is perhaps only the ultimate resemblance to the burned book, whose eternity each grain of sand enthrones for the abiding moment," he said.

THE SECOND TRIAL

How could this trial take place without defendants? The judges were facing their last sentence, facing themselves, alone with themselves in the desert they had withdrawn to.

One said—but to whom?—: *I have sentenced in the name of the Book, but I no longer know very well what a book is.*

Another said—but for whom did he intend it?—: *I have sentenced in the name of divine truth, but I no longer know very well what truth is.*

The third said—but addressed to whom?—: *I have sentenced, because I am Jewish, a Jew who has made unjustifiable pronouncements, but I no longer know very well what a Jew is.*

The fourth said—but for whom did he speak?—: *I have sentenced and by the fact of sentencing have become a pariah.*

How long will they ramble on like this between sky and sand? May their memory weaken and their eyes film over. The dark—did we not know this?—is a promise of nothingness.

*

Between one book and another there is an infinite desert peopled with thoughts, messianic hope, dreams, remorse, prayers, calls of distress or love; peopled with dead letters.

Now the moment has come when we too must measure ourselves against silence, against all that, within us, has spoken, acted and fallen silent for good.

A book is always approaching or prolonging a book half-glimpsed.

Do not try to read the desert. You would find all books buried in the dust of their words.

(The time of the book is the time of resemblance.
We have lived this time in every word.
The end of the book is perhaps the end of time.)

ABOUT THE AUTHOR

Edmond Jabès died in Paris in 1991 at the age of 78. He left his native Egypt during the Suez crisis of 1956 and settled in Paris. He is regarded as one of France's most important contemporary writers. His awards include the Prix des Critiques (1970), the Prize for Arts, Letters and Science of the Foundation of French Judaism (1982), the Grand Prix National de Poésie (1987), and the Italian Pasolini and Cittadella prizes (1983 and 1987). Wesleyan University Press has published in English the author's *The Book of Questions* (seven books in two volumes), *The Book of Dialogue* (1987), *The Book of Resemblances* (1990), and an anthology, *From the Book to the Book* (1991).

ABOUT THE TRANSLATOR

Rosmarie Waldrop's recent books of poetry are *Peculiar Motion*, *The Reproduction of Profiles*, and *Streets Enough to Welcome Snow*. She has also written novels, *The Hanky of Pippin's Daughter* and *A Form/of Taking/It All*. Her translations of Jabès have received a Columbia University Translation Center award.

ABOUT THE BOOK

The Book of Resemblances was composed on the Mergenthaler Linotron 202 in Caledonia, a typeface designed for Linotype in 1939 by W. A. Dwiggins, who named it Caledonia because of its derivation from the nineteenth-century typeface known as Scotch. The typesetter was Brevis Press of Bethany, Connecticut. The design is by Kachergis Book Design of Pittsboro, North Carolina.

University Press of New England
publishes books under its own imprint and is the publisher for Brandeis University
Press, Brown University Press, Clark University Press, University of Connecticut,
Dartmouth College, Middlebury College Press, University of New Hampshire, University of Rhode Island, Tufts University, University of Vermont, and Wesleyan
University Press.

Library of Congress Cataloging-in-Publication Data

Jabès, Edmond.
   [Soupçon, le désert. English]
   Intimations, the desert / Edmond Jabès ; translated from the
French by Rosmarie Waldrop.
      p.   cm. — (The book of resemblances ; 2)
   Translation of: Le soupçon, le désert.
   ISBN 0-8195-5240-2
   I. Title. II. Series: Jabès, Edmond. Livre des ressemblances.
English ; 2.
PQ2619.A112S613   1991
848'.91407—dc20   90-48669
             CIP